MONUMENT TO

COL. BENJAMIN BELLOWS.

IN THE CEMETERY AT WALPOLE, N.H.

[*Inscription on the south side of the Monument:*]

COL. BENJAMIN BELLOWS,

A WISE, COURAGEOUS, AND HONEST MAN,

BY A LARGE HOSPITALITY,

BY FAITHFULNESS AND ABILITY IN PUBLIC TRUSTS,

BY BRAVELY PROTECTING,

PRUDENTLY COUNSELLING, AND LIBERALLY AIDING

THE FRONTIER SETTLERS,

GAINED

THE RESPECT AND LOVE OF HIS CONTEMPORARIES,

AND MADE HIMSELF A PATTERN

FOR THOSE WHO SEEK TO BE

FATHERS OF COMMUNITIES.

[*Inscription on the north side:*]

TO THE MEMORY OF

BENJAMIN BELLOWS,

THE FOUNDER OF WALPOLE,

WHO DIED 10 JULY, 1777,

AGED SIXTY-TWO YEARS,

THIS MONUMENT WAS ERECTED

IN THE YEAR 1854,

BY HIS NUMEROUS DESCENDANTS.

(Medallion on the West Side.)

(On the East.)

HISTORICAL SKETCH

OF

COL. BENJAMIN BELLOWS,

FOUNDER OF WALPOLE:

AN ADDRESS,

ON OCCASION OF THE GATHERING OF HIS DESCENDANTS TO THE

CONSECRATION OF HIS MONUMENT,

AT WALPOLE, N. H., OCT. 11, 1854.

BY HENRY W. BELLOWS.

WITH AN APPENDIX,

CONTAINING AN ACCOUNT OF THE FAMILY MEETING.

NEW-YORK:
JOHN A. GRAY, PRINTER, 95 & 97 CLIFF STREET, COR. FRANKFORT.
1855.

ADDRESS

MADE IN THE BURIAL-GROUND AT THE

CONSECRATION OF THE MONUMENT.

KINSMEN AND FRIENDS OF THE BELLOWS RACE:

WE are assembled to honor the memory of our common progenitor, Col. BENJAMIN BELLOWS. More than a century a go he looked upon the hills and valleys that smile in our view, and beheld only a howling wilderness, given up to the bear and the wolf and the more merciless savage. His sagacious eye detected the fertility, the wealth, and the beauty that lay hid beneath a tangled forest, and selected and secured for his children's children this matchless portion of our native land. His brave arm occupied and defended this outpost of civilization when this whole frontier was blazing with the midnight conflagrations of the Indians' torch, when no man dared to labor without one hand on his musket, and no mother could sleep without starting and hugging her babe, as she dreamt of the whoop of the savage. His axe felled the primitive forest and laid open the fair meadows and the proud hills that make our beautiful town, while his industry, enterprise, and economy prepared the foundations of that agricultural wealth that has enriched his children, and made them an independent, a prosperous, and a happy family. His forecasting and judicious mind here laid the corner-stones of those religious, social, and political institutions, which have been the nourishment, the protection, and the happiness of successive generations. His personal integrity, blameless life, and respected character were the beginning of whatever honest pride of name, social respectability, and local influence our family have enjoyed. We gratefully hail him our founder; the original fountain of whatever worldly prosperity, public influence, or personal pride our race has known.

The founders of communities and of families have always enjoyed honor and commemoration among men. They necessarily possess superior and uncommon qualities. Striking out of the beaten track, they summon the heroic powers of our nature to their support, and draw upon the original resources of genius. They have energy to stamp their hand and their mind upon their times, and inscribe an ineffaceable writing upon some part of the edifice of society. Generations must elapse before we can distinguish the substantial from the merely showy men of the past. Those whose plans were prudent, whose native force was genuine and peculiar, whose blood was strong and pure, survive in the race they leave, in the communities they found, in the honor and esteem they receive. The ostentatious, the popular, and the brilliant have a great name in their day, and throw a brief lustre about their immediate descendants, but are speedily forgotten, while their names and places are filled by others; the solid, the useful, the substantial men rise into true honor, as their descendants prove the virtue of the blood and the value and permanency of the influences and possessions inherited from them.

This fresh and modest monument, which his numerous descendants have erected to their Founder, is more honorable to him to-day, than a column of a hundred feet would have been, raised at the time of his decease. That might have been the offering of fondness, the tribute paid to dazzling services in the field or the council-room, the reflection of party feeling, or temporary prejudice. We should probably have found it, to-day, in ruins—neglected and uncared for, or in ridiculous contrast with the actual reputation of him in whose honor it was built. But here, after his ashes have slept seventy-seven years in undistinguished simplicity, we gather to the spot, from every part of these United States—just born into existence when he died—to testify our fresh and growing sense of the honor and blessing of a descent from him; to declare and embody our declaration in marble, that time has tested and proved the worth and the strength of our Founder, and the original and lasting power he had of perpetuating himself; and to show that his name and praise are greater now than the day he died. It is a great thing to be remembered by successive generations, and to be remembered for civil services.

I congratulate you that the qualities and the reputation we commemorate by this monument are of so simple, pure, and permanent a character. It is no scarred and plumed warrior, no brilliant orator from the senate, no honor-laden civilian, whose names are written in their country's history, that this monument recalls. The plain farmer who trimmed a wilderness into a garden, who converted an unpeopled district into a populous town, and left a name for honor and purity, industry and sagacity, hospitality and public spirit to his children—the founder of a town and the head of a family, this is the unambitious and modest worth we come to commemorate. It is without detractors, without envy, and without jealousy that such mild honors are paid. Worth alone commands them, and they are not likely to be stolen away. It is honorable to him, it is honorable to us, the proceedings of this day. It is a useful and Christian example, thus to exalt the merit of modest and social services. When society honors good citizenship and domestic worth above the more popular qualities of martial or political success, it will be a good omen for civilization.

Kinsmen, we have cordially united in raising this commemorative stone. And it is not only a monument to our common ancestor, but, in some sort, a testimonial of respect and affection toward the numerous children of our venerated Father that sleep in this sacred inclosure—to the two mothers that cherished his immediate family, who now sleep by his side—and to his and their sons and daughters, all now gathered to their parents; again to their children, our immediate parents, kinsmen, children, slumbering in this great mound of family dust!

Over all this precious heap of ashes, once animated with his blood, sharing the advantages of his labors and good name, living on the spot he added to civilization—over all this memory-cherished dust, this monument stands guardian, ornament, and witness; and while it looks upon the graves of the generations of our race that are gone, it looks toward the place where the living generations dwell, to bless their prosperity, to chasten their conduct, to remind them of their obligations to their progenitor, and their debt to the grave.

> "Let not the dead forgotten lie,
> Lest men forget that they must die."

It is the warning written on his old grave-stone, and we are heeding its voice in thus renewing and adorning his memorial.

In erecting this monument, we invoke a fresh attention to our Founder, but also to ourselves. We make a claim, we assert a reputation, we publish our family union, our self-respect, our love of what is worthy, our desire to be known and remembered for integrity, hospitality, domestic worth, and public spirit. Shall we redeem the pledge which we are here giving this community?

Finally, we erect this monument to God, as a tribute of reverence, gratitude, and piety—for protecting our fathers in the days of peril and weakness; for blessing them with numerous offspring, and crowning them with competency and an honorable name. We mark with this white stone the happy day that sees so many of our family gathered on this favored spot, to acknowledge God's blessing on the labors and merits of our common Ancestor.

May this stone stand for ever! Let our children's careful hands keep it in repair from generation to generation. Let new honors, won for the name it bears, make its inscription more legible every day. Let it stand as long as the waters of yonder Falls—the liquid memorial of our Founder—continue to flow, recording his virtues for ever, as they hand down his name to all the successive generations of men.

HISTORICAL SKETCH.

ADDRESS IN THE TOWN-HALL.

Having solemnized the occasion which brought us together, with prayer and eulogy at the very grave of our Founder, I now invite the attention of his descendants and their friends assembled here, to a rapid survey of his history and that of his immediate children.

The first Bellows* of whom any trace can be found in Ame-

* The name, as we spell it, is still found in England, although it is rare. Thirty years and more ago, Mr. Abel Bellows met in Northampton, England, a gentleman, mayor of the city, who had married a lady of our name. The great London Post-Office Directory, which is as good a repertory of English names as one can well imagine, contains, however, no name precisely like ours. Bellews, Bellis, Bellas, Bellos, Bellasis, Beloes, are all found there, and I do not doubt that they are all corruptions of the same root, of which our name is itself a corruption. I have seen a highly respectable gentleman of the name of Bellas, from Pennsylvania, who bore so striking a resemblance to our family as to strengthen the suspicion of a common origin of the names. Mr. Herbert Bellows some years ago discovered, by the aid of a professional herald in Boston, that a family in Lancashire still existed, of great respectability, of the name of Bellowes, whose coat of arms he caused to be drawn out. I find, on further examination in the extensive heraldic treasures of the Astor Library, that the family of Bellewe, in Devonshire. in England, the Bellews of Barmeath, in Ireland, and the Bellowes of Lancashire, have, with slight differences, the same coat of arms and crest, indicating a common origin; and this origin is traced to a Norman family which came to England with William the Conqueror, of the name of de Belle Eau, pluralized in English precisely our name in sound.

The Parliamentary Gazetteer of Ireland (under Barmeath) says the Bellews came from Normandy with William the Conqueror, and filled the office of marshals in his army. Eighteen of their name were knight-bannerets in succession, during the middle ages, and several peers of their name appear in the rolls of Parliament; but

rica is a certain John Bellowes, who, it appears, by a record discovered by Mr. James Savage, in England, and published in the Mass. Historical Collection, vol. viii., third series, p. 255, embarked in the "Hopewell," of London, William Burdock master, for New-England, April 1, 1635. He is entered in the list of passengers as Jo(hn) Bellowes (aged) 12. In whose care the boy came, from what part of England, or what his early career in this country was, I am at present unable to state; but there is little doubt that he is the John Bellows who afterward married Mary Wood, at Concord, Mass., and who was the grandfather of our founder.

John Bellows and Mary Wood were married at Concord, Mass., May 9, 1655. They had ten children, the youngest of whom was Benjamin, born, probably, in 1677.*

owing to attainder in the civil wars, or failure of issue, they have not transmitted their titles to posterity.

The Bellews have, however, extensive estates in Louth and Galway; Sir Patrick Bellew, of Barmeath, being the head of the family in Ireland.

The English Bellews have their family seat at Bellew Court, in Stockley English, which they have owned about two hundred years. John Prestwood Bellew represents the family there.

The heraldic bearings of the English and Irish Bellews and the Bellowes of Lancashire are essentially the same.

The field or ground of the escutcheon is black, the bars interlaced are of a gold color, the chevron is blue, and bears three lions' heads (erased of the second) in gold. It is a highly honorable coat of arms.

The crest, however, is the most expressive and interesting part of it. It is thus described in Burke's Peerage:

"An arm embowed, habited, the hand proper grasping a chalice, pouring water (*belle eau*, in allusion to the name) into a basin, also proper. Motto, *Tout d'en haut*—All from on high."

Now the Irish Bellews have the same crest and the same motto, except that, with the true Irish love for a fight, the arm has dropped the cup and seized a sword. The retention of the same peculiar and expressive motto proves it to have the same origin with the English crest.

Whether the Lancashire Bellowes have adopted this crest or not, I can not discover; but it belongs to the escutcheon they use, and it is fair to claim it as our own.

It gives a poetical and mellifluous etymological origin and account of our family name, and harmonizes with the flow of the beautiful waters that, at the Great Fall, continue to murmur our founder's name.

* There are different accounts of the names and birth-place of their children; at least three lists of them to be found in different records. Mr. A. H. Ward, the careful annalist of Shrewsbury and the Ward family, says they had four children (the three first and the ninth) at Concord, and five at Marlborough, and that their names were

1. Mary, born 22d April, 1656.
2. Samuel, born 22d January, 1657; died at Marlborough, Sept. 29, 1680.
3. Abigail, born 6th May, 1661; married Isaac Lawrence, April 19, 1682.
4. Isaac, born 13th Sept., 1663.
5. John, born 13th May, 1666.
6. Thomas, born 7th Sept., 1668.

Benjamin,* the father of our *founder*, is said to have been adopted by one Benjamin Moore, of Lancaster, and to have inherited his fortune, which was, for the times, considerable. This fortune, it is also said, he afterward lost in a protracted lawsuit with a British officer. His substance and standing were, at any rate, such as to enable him to marry into a family of the greatest respectability. He was united, in 1704,† to the

7. Eleazer, born 13th April, 1671; married Esther Barrett, both of Marlborough, Oct. 11, 1692.

8. Daniel, born 15th March, 1672 or 3; died at Concord, July 20, 1676.

9. Nathaniel, born 3d April, 1676.

They also had *Benjamin*, but the date of his birth is not yet found recorded. The family, he adds, were driven from Marlborough at the breaking up of that town by the Indians, in 1675; they retired to Concord, and, in 1680, were again in Marlborough. Benjamin's name is not on the record of either of those towns. Shattuck in his History of Concord, says, John Bellows had children born from 1655 to 1679. He names some of them, and among them Benjamin; only four, and Benjamin last, as if tho youngest. Farmer says the same. Mr. Ward adds, There is no doubt in my mind but that the John Bellows who came in the "Hopewell," is the same who married Mary Wood. She was the daughter of John Wood (who died in Marlborough, July 10, 1678, aged 68) and Mary Wood, who died Aug. 17, 1690, aged 80. [Marlborough Rec.] John Bellows died at Marlborough, Jan. 10, 1683, age not recorded, but about 62, according to his age when he came over. His widow died Sept. 16, 1707, age not recorded—probably about 86.

* Uncle Peter, our founder's oldest son, told his son Solomon that, on a visit at Lunenberg, in the life-time of Col. Ben's father, he saw two brothers of his, one a small man, the other a very large one; one a resident of Pennsylvania, the other of New-York State. There are several branches of the family, severed before our Walpole founder's date, scattered over the United States, which it would be interesting to trace to their trunk.

† [*From a letter addressed to the author by Joseph Willard, Esq., of Boston.*]—Henry Willard—Dorcas Cutler, second wife. He was fourth son of Major Simeon Willard, and died in 1701, in Lancaster, where he had resided during the greater part of his life. In his will he names "Dorcas, my beloved wife," and constitutes her "sole executrix." There were six children of this marriage—perhaps seven. Two of them were men of mark, namely, Col. Samuel, of Lancaster, who commanded a regiment at Louisbourg, and Col. Josiah, a leader in the settlement of Lunenburg, Mass., and Winchester, N. H.

Dorcas was married to Willard probably about 1689—when her second husband, Benj. Bellows, was only thirteen years old—if Sibley is correct in the date of his birth. Perhaps you have the place of her birth; if not, I will hazard the *conjecture* that she was of Charlestown, then abounding in Cutlers—one of whom, namely, Hannah Cutler, became the wife of Daniel, brother of Henry Willard, Dec. 6, 1683.

Shattuck's "Concord" has the following: "John Bellows—Mary, daughter of John Wood, of Marlborough, 1655, and had Mary, Samuel, Abigail, Daniel, and *Benjamin*, born between 1655 and 1676. Removed to Marlborough, and some of his descendants to Walpole, N. H.

Benjamin, I presume, was born in Marlborough, None of the Bellows family "subscribed to the minister's house," in 1688, in Lancaster; nor are there any of the name in "the settlement of the garrisons" at that place, in 1692. Hence, as we may presume that the early Bellows were both generous and brave, we may equally well presume that they were not of L. in 1688, 1692.

The earliest notice I find of any of the name in L. is of Benjamin, in his early manhood. I find him there on the 18th of August, 1698, when he became the

widow Willard, whose maiden name was Dorcas Cutter. The Willards were then the principal family in Lancaster—Levi and Abel Willard being each distinguished in the legal pro-

purchaser of exceeding rich acres near the centre of that exceeding pleasant town. From 1698 to February, 1730, he appears as grantor or grantee in forty-two deeds, of which I have memoranda, and there are probably others.

In 1706 he sold the choice estate I have mentioned, and, in 1712, and also in 1727, I find him residing in the north-easterly part of Lancaster, at a place called "Still River," now a part of Harvard, where, in right of his wife, he rejoiced in the occupation of the fertile farm which had been the property of her first husband.

Benjamin lived in the valley of the Nashaway more than thirty years, and was pretty large landed proprietor.

In the last deed of which I have taken note, Feb. 30, 1730, he calls himself of Lunenburg.

In sundry suits he calls himself, or is called, of Lancaster: August, 1724 and 1726; March, 1727; December, 1727 and 1728. In another suit against him, December, 1728, he is called of Lunenburg, *alias* of Lancaster. In a suit, May, 1729, he is called of Lancaster. In 1730, [I believe,] in James Bowdoin's suit to recover possession of real estate mortgaged to him by Bellows, the latter is described as "resident in Lunenburg." In an action of debt brought against him in May, 1731, he is called of Lunenburg.

He was on the defendant side in divers actions for debt, and seems to have possessed more acres than pounds lawful. In one suit, 1712, he was defaulted; but, "being said to be in his majesty's service," the case was "continued till next terme."

In December, 1715, he sued Sheriff Gookin for an assault and battery, at Watertown, and imprisonment at Cambridge thirty hours. Gookin recovered in the C. C. Pleas, and Bellows appealed. Meanwhile B. was fined by the sessions for resisting the Sheriff, and appealed therefrom. I have not looked to ascertain what became of these appeals.

I have not the year when he married Mrs. Dorcas. She became a widow, I should say, about July, 1701. [Henry's will was proved Aug. 8, 1701.] I can not tell how long it was ere she dried her tears, doffed her weeds, and appeared as Mrs. Benjamin Bellows. All I can say is, that I first find her as his "married wife," July 12, 1705, and thence I trace her through various deeds, lovingly surrendering her right of dower, down to June 28, 1729.

Lancaster meeting-house was burnt by the Indians, and immediately the customary New-England discussion and controversy ensued touching the proper site for a new building. Leading men who lived at some distance from the old building, and who happened at the time to possess large local influence, were urgent for their own neighborhood. The trouble lasted through several years, and the authority of the Great and General Court was sought as in like cases elsewhere. Benjamin was among the petitioners for the old hallowed spot. The petitioners were on the west side of the river where "the meeting-house always stood." They "front towards the enemy, and have suffered very much, and are diminished in their number, several heads of families having been cut off within these few years. . . . Several families have removed for fear of the enemy, even to the bounds of Marlborough." They argue that if the new site should be taken, "the enemy might come when the inhabitants were att meeting, and destroy the whole western part, and secure the bridge, so that nobody should be able to resist them or relieve their friends; but the meeting-house being built on the west and exposed side, . . . the inhabitants on that side are a guard to the others on this side as well as to themselves; . . . they on this side, having never had a man killed in the service, are grown so numerous that they out-vote your petitioners and carry it against them at their town-meetings." Nov. 29, 1705, is the date of the petition.

There were several other petitions and remonstrances; but finally, in November, 1706, the Eastern party prevailed over Benjamin and his neighbors.

John Bellows was one of the proprietors of Marlborough at the time of its incor-

fession. Abel,* after whom our well-known kinsman of this town, now living, (Abel Bellows,) was named, was reputed a Tory, and obliged to flee to England on account of his anti-national principles. He returned, after the peace, and settled at Worcester. Levi† left his name to another uncle of mine, who died a bachelor—an unusual fate in the Bellows family.‡

The state of the country at the time of the marriage of our founder's father, in 1704, may be inferred from an old record, (see vol. ii. of the Historical Journal, N. H. Library, pp. 154, 155, 184,) by which we learn that, in the year 1711, there were no fewer than twenty-six garrison-houses within the limits of Marlborough, to each of which were assigned, on an average, five or six families—the whole number of families being one hundred and thirty-seven. This was done by act of the General Court of Massachusetts, entitled an act for the better security and defence of the frontiers. In a list of the garrison, given in the report of a committee, occur the names of two garrisoned houses, under control, one of Eliazar Bellows, one of John Bellows. These garrison-houses were usually common dwelling-houses, surrounded by palisades and furnished with a supply of fire-arms and ammunition. Who this Eliazar and this John Bellows were, it is difficult to say; but doubtless near relatives of our founder's father,§ and we may safely infer that our Walpole father's childhood was familiar with danger, and thoroughly prepared by early experience for the frontier-life he afterward encountered here.

Benjamin Bellows, son of Benjamin and Dorcas Bellows, was born May 26, 1712. His mother had by her first husband

poration in 1660. He was the one mentioned by Shattuck, and *probably* the John of 28 "Mass. Hist. Soc. Col." There was a John Bellows in the settling of the Marlborough garrisons, Dec. 11th, 1711, assigned to John Newton's (Jr.) garrison. Eleazer Bellows was a soldier in the same garrison.

* Abel, son of Joseph, son of the founder.

† Levi, son of Joseph, son of the founder.

‡ W. Lincoln's History of Worcester, p. 39, records a petition to Gov. Dudley, in 1709, and to the Council and Representatives, to have a firm foundation of a settlement laid, and a fort built, and needful protection, and (they) are willing to inhabit and settle the place. There are sixteen names to the petition, and Benjamin Bellows is the fourth name. This was undoubtedly our founder's father. Probably the petition was not granted, as the disturbed condition of public affairs often prevented the concurrence of the Council.

§ Own brother, it now appears.

three sons, whose history it is not to our present purpose to trace. She had by her second marriage only one son, our founder, and three daughters. The names of the children, of whom Benjamin was the youngest, were

Mary, born 1707, who married Moses Gould.

Juda, born 1708, who married Fairbanks Moore, afterward killed by the Indians.

Joanna, born 1710, who married Ephraim Wetherbee, and was settled in Charlestown, No. 4, and

Benjamin, born May 26, 1712.

His mother lived to old age, and died at Lunenberg, Sept. 8, 1747.

The town-records of Lunenburg contain abundant evidence of the public spirit and importance of both the father of our founder and the son.*

At how early a period the family moved into Lunenberg it is not easy to say; but from the position of the family homestead, in the very centre of the town, it is natural to conclude that the family was one of the earliest upon the ground. The house occupied by our Col. Bellows, and perhaps by his father before him, is still standing—the property of a daughter of Mr. Stearns, (a relative of the family)—occupied by Dr. King. Whether our founder inherited the Lunenberg place from his father, or earned it by his own exertions, I can not discover. Judging from the enterprise of his later years, we can not imagine him to have been idle until he was forty years old—the period of his removal to Walpole; and the probability is that this farm of eight hundred acres in Lunenberg was the result of his energetic industry. One of his grandchildren, now nearly four-score, recollects hearing that his grandfather, when a boy of fifteen, managed to buy a yoke of steers, and that, while yet a mere youth, he commenced earning his own living by teaming. However that was, it is certain that he pushed his course with such energy that, at the age of twenty-three, he was able to win and marry, Oct. 7, 1735, the sister of the first settled minister of Lunenberg, namely, Abigail

* A lot of land for the meeting-house in Lunenberg was bought of Benjamin Bellows, Jr., and T. Prentice; and old Mr. Esek Whiting, a very venerable citizen there, remembers that Col. Bellows gave in his part of it, though Mr. Prentice took pay for his. The town voted, Nov. 19, 1750, £11 16s. 8d. toward the payment.

Stearns, whose other sisters married, one, Col. Joseph Blanchard, of Dunstable, and the other, Col. Willard.

It is difficult or impossible to obtain any account of Col. Bellows's life in Lunenberg. He came on to the stage at a period when the colonies were poor and struggling for existence. Six successive wars, it will be remembered, desolated the country and its spare inhabitants in its colonial state.

I. The Pequot war, the great burden of which fell on Massachusetts and Connecticut, Connecticut being the scene of operations. It commenced in May, 1637, and ended September, 1638.

II. Philip's war, which commenced in June, 1675, and lasted three years. Six hundred of the inhabitants of New-England were cut off, twelve or thirteen towns utterly destroyed, and six hundred buildings consumed by fire. It is computed that about one man in eleven out of all capable of bearing arms was killed, and every eleventh family burnt out; that one eleventh of the whole militia and of all the buildings of the United Colony were swept off by this war.

III. King William's war, which commenced in 1688, and, with brief intervals, continued ten years. This war was carried on against the colonies by the Indians and the Canadian French. Besides pillaging and burning houses, and killing the inhabitants, numerous families were carried captives to Canada, and sold there. At seasons of this war the people were almost wholly dispirited with the prospect of poverty and ruin.

IV. Queen Anne's war, which commenced in 1703 and closed in 1713. The foes were the same as in the last war. The inhabitants were constantly harassed with calls to military service; agriculture was neglected, many people killed and captured, and a heavy public debt incurred.

V. The Three Years', or Lovewell's war, which was declared in 1722 and closed in 1726. The burden of this fell upon the eastern townships of Massachusetts and New-Hampshire. Mr. Blanchard, of Dunstable, the ancestor, I suppose, of Col. Blanchard, of the same place, brother-in-law of Col. Bellows, was carried away captive in this war.

VI. Lastly. The second French war, which grew out of a rupture between England and France, in which, of course, their respective colonies were compelled to take part. It commenced in 1744, and closed in 1763, covering eight years of Col. Bellows's life in Lunenberg, and eleven of his life in Walpole. New-Hampshire furnished five hundred men, one eighth of the whole land force, in the important and successful expedition against the city and fortress of Louisburg, in Cape Breton; the capture of which filled America with joy, and Europe with astonishment. One Henry Bellows (it appears) commanded the British ship Dispatch in the expedition against Cape Breton, and served subsequently in the war against France and the Indians. He was granted a tract of 5826 acres, situated east of Conway, by Gov. Wentworth, November 13, 1772.*

Of the one thousand men raised in the counties of Worcester and Hampshire, in the year 1756, to succor Gen. Winslow against the French and Indians, five men went from what is now Paxton, originally belonging to Rutland and Leicester, Mass. Among them were Ezekiel Bellows, etc. They were under Gen. Ruggles's command, and a part, if not the whole, were employed at Crown Point, Ticonderoga, and Fort Edward, at different times during the war.†

There can be little doubt from Col. Bellows's after-life, that during this period, when the country was poor, drained of able-bodied men, constantly called on for supplies of food to support the army, and with little prospect of a settled government, that he, who manifestly held an important place in his native town, was subject to all the difficulties, discouragements, and delays of the times, and that he pursued his farming a good deal with reference to the public life of the country, raising supplies for the army, and probably, from his rank as Colonel, which he brought with him to Walpole, doing his part toward raising and drilling the men constantly called for by the provincial authorities. It is likely that his son Joseph, who inherited the paternal estate, also inherited the paternal mode of business, and we know that he was constantly engaged in meeting the demands of the government for men and provisions.

* Vol. 2, Farmer & Moore's Historical Collections.

† Vol. 2, Historical Journal, p. 236, (New-Hampshire Collection, Concord,) History of Paxton.

Whenever war left any opportunities of enterprise, the exploration and survey of unoccupied lands was the business of every leading man on the frontier. Lunenberg was a frontier town, and Col. Bellows, as a man of ability, energy, and ambition, made that, doubtless, a great part of his business. He probably had no special education as a surveyor, but possessed general knowledge and tact sufficient to discharge the practical duties of this office. In those early times men served short apprenticeships, and constituted themselves offhand, whatever the necessities of the time called on them to be.

We now approach the period when Col. Bellows came to Walpole. From a very early time, settlements had been made on the lower parts of the Connecticut River, and had gradually crept up as far as Northfield on this side the river. Fort Dummer, on the other side of the river, was built in 1723 or 1724, on lands granted by Gov. Benning Wentworth. A petition is on file at the Massachusetts State House, file No. 7, signed by Bellows, Willard, and Boynton, asking, in 1736, for four hundred and fifty acres of land for a road from Lunenberg to Northfield. So that it seems that Col. Bellows's father must have turned his thoughts this way at a very early period. Keene was settled in the year 1734; but, from the terrible depredations of the savages, it was abandoned in 1747, and not again settled until 1750 or 1751. In 1752, eight or ten dwelling-houses had been erected there.* There is evidence that in the journeys made during King William's war in 1688 and onward, between Lake Champlain and Massachusetts, the fertility and value of the lands on Connecticut River, and particularly in the neighborhood of the *Great Fall*, had been carefully observed. Gov. Belcher obtained leave, for services rendered by his brother Andrew, in the Canada expedition of 1690, to survey and lay out in two pieces one thousand acres of unappropriated lands of the Province. The date of this consent was December 11, 1734. Another order was passed relative to the same, January 12, 1735, and certain lands were assigned to him, thus described: as "Two plots of land, on Connecticut River, laid out by Thomas Hinsdale and chainman

* Hale's Keene, p. 28.

on oath, containing in the whole one thousand acres, intended for fulfilling a grant made by this Court in the year 1734 to his Excellency, Jonathan Belcher, Esq.; the larger tract, containing six hundred acres and beginning at two butternut trees, marked + B, and attaining on Connecticut River at the lower end of the *third interval meadow on the east side of the river from Cold River;* thence east one hundred and thirty-four perch to a corner; thence north four hundred and seventy perch to another corner; then west ninety-five perch to a butternut tree, marked + B, on the bank of the river, and from thence down along the river to the butternut tree, where it began."* The other lot is on the west side of the river. November 30, 1736, it appears by a report on towns upon Connecticut River, that Nos. 1, 2, 3, and 5 were admitted as townships, and that sixty grantees were admitted and gave their bonds at Concord in 1736, (September.†)

Most of these townships laid out in 1736 were not occupied, and there is no evidence that the original grantees of No. 2, —which we suppose in this enumeration (different from one afterward made according to forts, by which it was called No. 3) to be Walpole—complied with the conditions. It is very certain that a grant of No. 2 was made to Nathaniel Harris and others, and it is probable that Gov. Belcher conveyed his right to them. Mr. Charles Lincoln informs me that a plan of Walpole, as granted to Willard, Bellows, and others in 1736, is in file No. 7 at the Massachusetts State House. Josiah Willard, it appears, was one of the committee‡ appointed January 16, 1736, to lay out towns on the Connecticut River, and this Bellows must have been Col. Bellows's father; so that we begin to see that our founder was carrying out a family purpose when he came to Walpole in 1752. He had doubtless thoroughly explored this region, and knew precisely what he was about when he procured the charter under which Walpole was finally settled.

* See Court Records, vol. 16, p. 256, also p. 85, also p. 262.

† P. 373, vol. 16, Court Records.

‡ The members of the Committee were Joseph Gerrish, Benjamin Prescott, *Josiah Willard,** Job Almy, Moses Pierson, and Capt. Joseph Gold. P. 282, 16 vol., Court Records, Massachusetts.

* Josiah Willard, (or was it his son?) afterward Sheriff and Recorder of Deeds of Cheshire county, under the laws of the province.

At the time when there was some controversy between New-Hampshire and Massachusetts, as to their boundary line, (prior to 1750,) a commissioner and an engineer or surveyor were appointed by each State, to meet together, run out, and settle the division-line. Col. Benjamin Bellows, of Lunenberg, Mass., was appointed the surveyor on the part of Massachusetts. This brought Col. Bellows into communication with Gov. Benning Wentworth, of New-Hampshire, who was pleased with Col. B., and wished to persuade him to settle in New-Hampshire. In order to do so, he offered him his choice of the unappropriated townships. Col. B. finally concluded to accept the offer, and came up into New-Hampshire to make his selection. Of the river-townships that he visited, he was convinced that the township now called Claremont would be the best purchase, as from its superior water-power, it was destined to be a populous and thriving place; but lying north of Fort No. 4, (Charlestown,) which was then the most northerly settlement, any body of men bold enough to locate there would be directly exposed to the attacks of the Indians, and would have to endure the brunt of their assaults. But the township now called Walpole pleased him, from the character of its soil and the beauty of its situation; and lying between Charlestown No. 4 and Fort Dummer, it would have superior advantages of security against the assaults of the Indians—a foe then much dreaded, from their numbers and treacherous character.

Col. B. purchased this township in conjunction with Col. Theodore Atkinson and Col. Jonathan Blanchard, (the latter a brother-in-law of Col. B.'s; they married sisters.)

Col. B. removed from Lunenberg to the new settlement in 1752, built a fort there, and organized a town-government.

The immediate reason for his leaving Lunenberg, according to a family tradition, is that he had become embarrassed by being bound for others, and in the great scarcity of money was unable to meet the demands. It is said, how truly I can not tell, that he was pursued by the sheriff to the line, and, once fairly over it, then and there stopped to parley with him, saying that he had no disposition to avoid his obligations, but a jail was a poor place in which to find the means of meeting them; that he would soon return and liquidate his debts. If the other part of the story be true, it is certain that he did this, as he continued to own, to the time of his death, and was able to bequeath to his son Joseph, the valuable estate he originally possessed in Lunenberg.

The charter under which Col. Bellows obtained Walpole is as follows:

"George II., by advice of Benning Wentworth, Governor, granted unto his loving subjects, inhabitants of New-Hampshire, and his majesty's other governments, in equal shares, whose names are entered on this grant, to be divided among them in sixty-seven equal shares, all that tract of land in said province of New-Hampshire described, etc., etc. And the same is incorporated as Walpole, and inhabitants therof are enfranchised and declared entitled to the privileges of other towns in said province, and as soon as there shall be fifty families resident there, shall have the liberty of holding two fairs annually, and shall also have a market opened and kept one or more days in each week, as may be thought advantageous. The first meeting of said town shall be held third Wednesday of March next, (1752,) and Benj. Bellows is appointed moderator of such meeting, and to call the same.

"To hold said land upon these conditions, namely, every grantee shall, within five years, cultivate five acres of land for every fifty acres of his share, and shall continue to improve and settle the same by additional cultivation, on penalty of forfeiture of his share.

"That all white and other pine-trees, fit for our royal navy, be preserved for use, and none be cut or felled without his majesty's special license, upon same forfeiture and punishment of any acts of parliament now or hereafter enacted.

"That before division of land, a tract or centre of township shall be marked in town-lots, one of which shall be allotted to each grantee, of the contents of one acre, yielding and paying therefor to us, etc., for ten years, one ear of Indian corn, annually, on first day of January, if lawfully demanded.

"Every proprietor, settler, or inhabitant shall yield and pay us, etc., yearly, after the expiration of ten years, one shilling, proclamation money, for every hundred acres he so owns, settles, or possesses, and so in proportion for greater or less tracts, which said money shall be paid to our council-chamber, or to officers appointed to receive it.

(Signed by) "BENNING WENTWORTH,

"In testimony, etc., Feb. 13, 1752, and twenty-fifth year of George's reign.
"Recorded by THEODORE ATKINSON, Sec."

A plan of the town accompanies the original charter. Nine years afterward, the following entry is made: (Lib. 1, Charter Records, fol. 229.) "The grantees having represented that, by reason of Indian wars, it has become impracticable to comply with the conditions of the grant. The time is lengthened one year, and one year thereafter annually, until our plenary instructions shall be received. Dated March 12, 1761. First year of George III."

There can be no doubt that Col. Bellows had acquaintance with this tract of country, and had fixed upon the neighborhood of *the Falls* as a place of ultimate settlement, long before the date of the charter. The great fall now known by his name, must itself have given to the tract immediately below it an importance to every practical inspector of lands which belonged to nothing else on the river, this side of the lower falls at Hadley. Great reference was had, in the early settlements, to the ultimate capabilities of townships, and the admirable fisheries of salmon and shad at the Great Falls—shad not being able to get above them, and salmon being most conveniently taken there—gave obvious importance to the site. There is reason to think that, in some manner, No. 2, then called Great Fall, was also known as Bellowstown, from a period ten or fifteen years before the actual settlement under the charter.

Parson Fessenden, of this town, in his letter to Jeremy Belknap, Jan. 22, 1791, says that "One family settled here in the spring of 1749, under the Bay claim. But the Hampshire proprietors began in 1742, and in 1753 Col. Benjamin Bellows moved his family into town; when the French war beginning soon after, he was obliged to fortify and live in a garrison."

This family is well known to be that of Mr. John Kilburn, and consisted of himself and Ruth Kilburn, his wife; Mehitable, his daughter; and John, his son. We shall hear more of them by and by.

The first town-meeting, doubtless to fulfill the letter of the charter, was held on the third Wednesday of March, 1752. Benjamin Bellows was appointed moderator and town-clerk, to both which offices he had served an apprenticeship at Lunenberg, being town-clerk there in 1739–40; and Theodore Atkinson, Esq., Joseph Blanchard, Esq., and Benjamin Bellows, selectmen. In the following year, precisely the same record is repeated; and so evidently is the ink drawn from the same horn, and the handwriting of one stroke, that it is impossible not to suspect that both records were made at the same time, and probably not till some years after they occurred.* Indeed, when we come to examine the appointments, and find Theodore Atkinson and Joseph Blanchard chosen selectmen—men who never lived in Walpole, or had any intention of doing so, but who had united with Col. Bellows in purchasing the grant —we begin to suspect that the only persons présent at the two first town-meetings were Col. Benj. Bellows, moderator—Col. Benj. Bellows, town-clerk—Col. Benj. Bellows, selectman; and that, in all probability, the town-meeting was held in bed, as the most comfortable place for the civic duties of the infant town.

Theodore Atkinson, Esq., whose home was in Londonderry, was the Secretary of the Province; a man of much weight and influence, who had given his name to one of the eastern towns of the State. Col. Blanchard was a brother-in-law of Col. Bellows, and lived at Dunstable. They had probably united in the purchase mainly out of friendship to Col. Bellows. Col. Blanchard being his brother-in-law, and a man of influence and means, it is well known, assisted him for many years in his money arrangements, and their final account was not settled until very shortly before Col. Bellows's death. As soon as he was able, our founder purchased both Atkinson's and Blanchard's rights, with the exception of a portion of Derry hill and the Boggy-meadow farm, early valued for its capabilities. The original deed of 19th April, 1760, is now before me, in which Rebecca Blanchard, of Dunstable, makes over, for sixty pounds sterling, four full rights or shares in said Walpole, granted to Stanton Prentice, Joseph Wynn, Joseph Blodget, and Sampson French; from which it appears that, in all probability, Bellows, Blanchard, and Atkinson purchased the rights of the larger part of the original grantees, very few of whom, it is certain, ever came to Walpole; and that, afterward, Col. Bellows bought out the other two principal proprietors. We may infer, too, that in 1760, the ordinary value put upon one sixty-eighth part of the grant was fifteen pounds sterling, which would make the whole worth about £1020, or $5000, then at least five times as much as it is now.

* They may have been copied from an older record-book by the Colonel.

According to the usual order, (although it does not appear in the charter,) a right of five hundred acres was reserved for the Governor, a lot to belong to the first settled minister as a sort of bounty, and a lot for a parsonage. There was also another reservation, the reference to which in the town records puzzled me, until I found out its nature. The record (January 1783) is this: "Voted to sell so much of the right for propagation of the Gospel in foreign parts, in the town of Walpole, as to pay Rev. Thomas Fessenden the arrearage of his salary the town owes him." Benning Wentworth, it seems, was a warm Church-of-England man, and to increase the funds of the Missionary Society in England, reserved in every town one right for the advantage of its treasury. It is pretty certain that the Missionary Society never derived any advantage from its claims, as they were quashed by the Revolutionary war before they had been made available. It is said that Governor Wentworth, in making his selection of land in Walpole, consulted Colonel Bellows as to what was the most favorable portion of the town to lay claim to; expressing his own decided preference for five hundred acres in the immediate neighborhood of the Great Fall, as the probable site of the future settlement. The Colonel very honestly told him that the land thereabout would make a very good calf-pasture, but nothing better. The Governor, perhaps imagining that the Colonel wished to appropriate these lands to himself, and so discouraged his own selection of them, at once resolved to lay his claim there; and his five hundred acres on the stony flanks of Fall Mountain were for some time jocosely called "the Governor's calf-pasture."

Governor Wentworth, says the historian of Keene, was fond of complimenting his noble friends in England, by scattering their names over New-Hampshire and Vermont. He called the first chartered town in Vermont, Bennington, after himself. Keene was named after a Sir Benjamin Keene, then minister from England to Spain. Westmoreland and Westminster were both called from English lords of that name, and Walpole, for Sir Robert Walpole, Prime Minister of George I. Charlestown derived its name from Sir Charles Knowles, who was in command of a ship in Boston at the time of Stevens's brave fight at No. 4, and testified his admiration of Stevens's courage by the gift of a handsome sword, and in turn was made godfather to the town.

Colonel Bellows was not so exclusively occupied with his settlement here as not to have an interest in the neighboring country. He called the first meeting of the proprietors and inhabitants of Keene in 1753, under Governor Wentworth's charter; at which meeting one hundred and twenty-two Spanish milled dollars were voted him, for his services and expenses in obtaining the charter. It is known, too, from the records of those towns, that he surveyed and laid out the towns of Rindge and Claremont.

Walpole did not grow so fast that Colonel Bellows was overwhelmed with business. Parson Fessenden says, that only four families settled in town until after the reduction of Canada in 1759. This accounts for the extraordinary number of offices that the Colonel himself filled, being appointed in 1755 and 1756 moderator, selectman, town clerk, town treasurer, surveyor of highways, etc.

In 1754, (the third year,) Samuel Johnson and Robert Powker, persons of whom I can learn nothing further, and somewhat doubt their personal presence, or corporal attention to their duties, are selectmen. The next year, Mr. John Kilburn is chosen, a *bona-fide* man, whose non-appearance before, in the great scarcity of citizens, increases my skepticism as to the actuality of the early town-meetings. The following year (1755) poor Mr. Twichel is joined with Mr. Kilburn. In 1756 Mr. Nathan Powers and Mr. Joseph Wood appear on the records, one as selectman, the other as constable. In 1757, every body seems to be frightened away but brave Kilburn and Colonel Bellows. So it is in 1758. In 1759, Mr. John Hastings, and Mr. Fairbanks Moore, who had married the Colonel's sister, and was afterwards killed by the Indians, take their places among the selectmen, and Benjamin Bellows, Jr., relieves his father of the laborious duties of town clerk, an office which he held from that time until 1795, when he was succeeded by Nicanor Townsley, being a period of thirty-six years.

Mr. Fessenden, who ought to be good authority, says that Colonel Bellows moved his family to Walpole in 1753. The family at that time consisted of his wife and five children:

Abigail,	born	December 21,	1736
Peter,	"	January 6,	1739
Benjamin,	"	October 6,	1740
John,	"	November 3,	1742
Joseph,	"	June 6,	1744.

His daughter, the oldest of the family, died at the age of twenty, while on a visit to Northfield, where her grave is yet marked with its stone—a terrible loss at that time, doubtless. Peter was fourteen years old, and Benjamin thirteen, when their father moved to Walpole; and Benjamin at nineteen was made town clerk, and Peter at twenty-one was chosen constable. So early was it necessary to force the duties of manhood on the boys of the family. The mother, Abigail Stearns, whether from grief at her daughter's loss the year before, or the hardships in her new life, died November 8, 1757, and was the first tenant of the burial ground. Peace to her ashes! Mother of so many of our race, who now lie by her side, and of so many who still live to praise her. She had an excellent repute for energy, piety, and motherly love, and her dust sweetly consecrated the spot, wherein her race was afterwards to repose.*

When Colonel Bellows came to Walpole, he found John Kilburn in a garrisoned house, of a small capacity, situated near Cold River, about two miles from the present centre of the town, on the road to the Falls, the exact spot being said to be just where two apple-trees, very visible on the east of the wayside, now bear the fruits of peace. The occasion of this defence was the incursions of the savages from the Canadian frontier. By the repeated wars of the preceding half-century, the Indians had been gradually driven further and further from the settlements of the English, and, I suppose, had not held a regular home in any portion of the Connecticut valley for many years. The original Indians of this neighborhood were all comprehended by the French under the name of the Abenaquis; from which we have taken the title of our mineral

* The church record at Lunenberg, Mass., under date of December 6, 1736, shows that Abigail Bellows, the wife of Benjamin Bellows, Jr., was then received into church communion, being recommended from the Church of Christ in Watertown. Notices are also found there of the baptism of five or six of the children of Benjamin and Abigail.

spring. They remembered, however, their old fishing and hunting-grounds, and were familiar with all the easiest passes between Canada and the English settlements. Evidences enough remain of their ancient use of this very soil; and the favorite spots of their sojourn are marked with accumulations of clam-shells, with arrow-heads, spear-heads, pestles and mortars, occasionally by human bones, turned up by the plough and spade of our civilization. The savages, in the intervals of their successive wars with the colonists, were in the habit of mixing more or less with the whites; caught their language and borrowed many of their ways, both good and evil; and in the occasional injuries they suffered in their dealings with the cupidity of the whites, were laid the foundations of many of the surprises, massacres, and captures they practised when the hour of war came. Their assaults on Keene, Deerfield, on Fort Dummer, and other places down the river, showed well enough what this settlement had to fear from them. A temporary peace had encouraged both Kilburn and Colonel Bellows to venture upon this exposed position, but they soon had abundant indications of the necessity of fortifying themselves.

Col. Bellows's fort, according to the account of "the 'Squire" who described it on the spot to Rev. Mr. Knapp, was situated a little north of his dwelling-house, (built in 1762, and still standing,) just on the brow of the terrace overlooking his magnificent meadows. It was shaped like an L, about a hundred feet long in the arms and twenty feet broad, built of logs and earth, and surrounded by an outer palisade. Although a private garrisoned house, it was yet of such importance as to be named among the fortresses maintained at the public expense at Fort Dummer, Westmoreland, and Charlestown, being No. 3 in this chain of defences. The royal government supplied each of these forts with an heavy iron gun for the public protection. Whether Col. Bellows drew any ammunition or men for his garrisoned house, as Hinsdale and Charlestown did, I can not certainly tell. But the only letter of his extant, to the best of my knowledge, is one which throws a ray of light on the subject. It is dated Westmoreland, August 31, 1754, and is addressed to his brother-in-law, Col. Joseph Blanchard, who had active command of a regiment in the lower part of the State. It is too interesting and solitary in its character not to be quoted in full. Thus it runs:

"SIR: We have the news from Charlestown, that on Thursday morning, the 29th of this instant, the Indians came to the house of James Johnson, and broke in and took sd Johnson, his wife and three children, and a maid and one Ebenr. Farnsworth and one Labbaree, and they suppose they have carried them all off; they have not found any of them killed. The people are in great distress all down the river, and at Keene and at Swanzey, and the few men sent will not more than supply one town, and the people can not secure their grain, nor hardly keep their garrison, etc.

"WESTMORELAND, *Aug.* 31, 1754. BENJ. BELLOWS.

"P S.—I have got no further than Westmoreland when I wrote this, and got all the men safe there. B. B."

It would appear that apprehensive of danger, Col. Bellows had been recruiting men from below for the defence of the settlements. He speaks as if he felt himself a kind of father of the country round about, and as if they would look to him to provide for their protection. I suppose he writes to Col. Blanchard in an official capacity, as his letter possesses none, of the familiarity of a brother-in-law's correspondence. It shows plainly enough the terrible apprehensions under which the settlers lived. This foray of the savages into Charlestown, with the captivity of Mrs. Johnson—the day but one before the date of this letter—gave rise to one of the most celebrated memoirs of Indian cruelty and heroic endurance on the part of its victim, ever furnished from that fascinating sort of annals. Dr. Dwight's account of Mrs. Jemima Howe's capture at Vernon in 1755, forms a pendant to the other picture.

Col. Bellows's apprehensions were destined to be very shortly realized. Two men, by name Daniel Twichel and Mr. Flynt, in the summer of 1755, (somewhere between the third Wednesday in March, 1755, when Daniel Twichel was appointed selectman, and the 17th August, when the Kilburn fight took place, but probably in August,*) had gone back to the hills, about a mile and a half north-east, on what is now the Drewsville road, to procure some timber for oars. Here they were shot by the Indians; one of them was scalped, the other cut open, his heart taken out and laid in pieces upon his

* Fessenden says a week before the Kilburn fight.

breast. This was the first Christian blood spilt in Walpole. The bodies were buried on the spot, which is accurately pointed out at this day. This event made a solemn impression on the settlers. They imagined that Twichel's spirit continued to hover over them, warning them of the wiles of the savages, and crying for vengeance on them. A remarkable rock in Connecticut River, where he used to fish with unfailing success, was for a long time held in religious veneration; and anglers are still tempted to Twichel's Rock as to a place where their luck is under the propitious influences of his memory.

Shortly before this, an Indian by the name of Philip had visited Kilburn's house in a friendly way, pretending to be in want of provisions. He was supplied with flints, flour, etc., and dismissed. Soon after it was ascertained that this same Indian had visited all the settlements on the river, doubtless to procure information of the state of their defences. Gov. Shirley about this time sent information to all the forts in this region, that five hundred Indians were collecting in Canada, whose aim was the butchery and extinction of the whole white population on the river. Greatly alarmed, the sparse population, unwilling to abandon their crops, had strengthened their feeble garrisons, and bravely determined to stand by their rude but promising homes.

Col. Benjamin Bellows had at this time about thirty men at his fort, about half a mile south of Kilburn's house, but too distant from it to afford him any aid. About noon on the 17th of August, 1755, Kilburn and his son John, in his eighteenth year, a man by the name of Peak and his son, were returning home to dinner from the field, when one of them discovered the red legs of the Indians among the alders, "as thick as grasshoppers." They instantly made for the house, fastened the door, and prepared for an obstinate defense. Kilburn's wife Ruth and his daughter Hetty, were already in the house. In about fifteen minutes, the savages were seen crawling up the bank east of the house, and as they crossed a foot-path, one by one, one hundred and ninety-seven were counted; about the same number, it afterwards proved, had remained in ambush, near the mouth of Cold River, but joined the attacking party soon.

The savages appeared to have learned that Col. Bellows and

his men were at work at his mill about a mile east, (on what is called the Blanchard Brook, near where it is crossed by the Drewsville road, it being built at that distance from the fort on account of the convenience of a water-fall,) and they intended to waylay and murder them before attacking Kilburn's house. Col. Bellows and his men were now returning home, each with a bag of meal on his back, when the dogs began to growl and betray the neighborhood of an enemy. The Colonel, knowing the language of the dogs and the wiles of the Indians, instantly adopted his policy. He directed his men, throwing off the meal, to crawl carefully to the rise of the land, and on reaching the top of the bank, to spring together to their feet, give one whoop, and instantly drop into the sweet fern. This manœuvre had the desired effect to draw the Indians from their ambush. At the sound of the whoop, fancying themselves discovered, the whole body of the savages arose from the bushes in a semi-circle round the path Col. Bellows was to have followed. His men improved instantly the excellent opportunity for a shot offered by the enemy, who were so disconcerted, that without firing a gun, they darted into the bushes and disappeared. The Colonel, sensible of his unequal force, hurried his men off by the shortest cut to the fort, and prepared for its defence.

The cowardly savages had, however, no intention of coming again into the range of his guns. They determined to take their vengeance out of a weaker party, and soon after appeared on the eminence east of Kilburn's house. Here the same treacherous Philip, who had visited him and partaken his hospitality so short a time before, came forward under shelter of a tree and summoned the little garrison to surrender. "Old John, Young John," was his cry, "I know ye; come out here. We give you good quarter." "Quarter!" vociferated old Kilburn, in a voice of thunder. "You black rascals, begone, or we'll *quarter* you." It was a brave reply for four men to make to four hundred! Philip returned, and after a short consultation, the war-whoop rang out, as if, to use the language of an ear-witness, "all the devils in hell had been let loose." Kilburn was lucky and prudent enough to get the first fire, before the smoke of the battle perplexed his aim, and was confident he saw Philip himself fall. The fire from the little garrison was returned by a shower of balls from the savages, who rushed forward to the attack. The roof was a perfect "riddle-seive." Some of the Indians fell at once to butchering the cattle, others to a wanton destruction of the grain, while the larger part kept up an incessant fire at the house. Meanwhile, Kilburn and his men—aye, and his women—were all busily at work. Their powder they poured into their hats for greater convenience; the women loaded the guns, of which they had several spare ones—all of them being kept hot by incessant use. As their stock of lead grew short, they suspended blankets over their heads to catch the balls of the enemy, which penetrated one side of the roof and fell short of the other. These were immediately run by these Spartan women into bullets, and before they had time to cool, were sent back to the enemy, from whom they came. Think ye, fair dames of Walpole in 1854, could your delicate nerves command the hot ladle, and load the murderous gun, while four hundred savages were shouting for your blood on the other side of a frail palisade of logs? Several attempts were made to force the door, but the unerring aim of the marksmen within sent such certain death to these assailants, that they soon desisted from their efforts. Most of the time the Indians kept behind logs and stumps, and avoided, as they best could, the fire of the little Gibraltar. The whole afternoon, even till sun-down, the battle continued, until, as the sun set, the savages, unable to conquer so small a fortress, discouraged and baffled, forsook the ground, and, as was supposed, returned to Canada, abandoning the expedition on which they had set out. It is not unreasonable to suppose that their fatal experience here, through the matchless defence of those Walpole heroes and heroines, was instrumental in saving hundreds of the dwellers on the frontier from the horrors of an Indian massacre.

Seldom did it fall to the lot of our forefathers to win a more brilliant crown than John Kilburn earned in this glorious exploit. Peak got the only wound of his party, receiving a ball in the hip, from exposure at a port-hole, which unhappily, for lack of surgical care, caused his death on the fifth day. The Indians never again appeared in Walpole, although the war did not terminate until eight years afterwards. John Kilburn lived to see his fourth generation on the stage, and enjoying the benefits of a high civilization on the spot he had rescued from the savages. He possessed an honest heart, lived uprightly, and died in peace. A plain stone in Walpole burying-ground thus commemorates his departure, and speaks his eulogy in a brief, expressive phrase:

IN MEMORY
OF
JOHN KILBURN,
Who departed this life for a better
APRIL 8, 1789,
In the 85th year of his age.
He was the first settler of this town in
1749.

In 1814, his son, young John, last visited the scene of his youthful exploits. He died among his children, in Shrewsbury, Vt., in 1822. One of his sons died in this town only a year or two since.

What amount of destruction Kilburn made among the savages it was impossible to tell, as it is well known they carefully carry off and conceal their dead. It is said that Indian graves have been dug up at Cold River, and on the line of the railroad in that neighborhood, and six graves were found on the site of the Island House at the Falls, in 1833, which may possibly have been those of victims in this fight.

Life in the fort during the first eight years of Col. Bellows's residence in Walpole, must have been excessively anxious and laborious. It was impossible to proceed to any kind of labor without carrying arms, and sufficient company for protection. Meanwhile, however, food had to be provided, and cattle and corn must be raised. Before he built his mill, the Colonel was obliged to carry his corn to Northampton to be ground, going down in boats in the spring, and returning with meal and other stores. A kind of watch-tower was erected outside of the fort, by timbers leaning against a great elm, near where the barn on the east side of the road now stands, in which a look-out was kept. The Colonel was very strict, and would allow none of his men to be out of the fort after dark. It is said, however, that Ben, when a boy of eighteen, being placed on the watch, was beguiled to leave his post, to get some water-melons from the patch in the meadow; that in his rambles he fell in with evidences of Indians in the immediate neighborhood, and betook himself to the bank of the river, the enemy lying between him and the fort. There he lay concealed, afraid to stir, all night and all next day, to the great consternation of the family, who did not dare to venture out in search of him. Happily, he returned safe before the next night, cured of his love of water-melons.

Before the year 1761, there was so little that could be done in Walpole, except hold the place—such was the reluctance of settlers to venture into a region of so much peril—that Colonel Bellows probably absented himself at various times, as it appears he did in 1754, on excursions to his farm in Lunenberg, which had still to be carried on, and in pursuing his business as a surveyor. I find a charge which he makes for victualling and harboring troops, on their way to Canada, which makes it probable enough that his fort was not seldom a point aimed at by soldiers, then in constant motion between the Bay State and Canada. It is likely, too, that the fort was a depository of provisions for the settlers scattered through the neighboring towns. Certainly later, if not at this early time, he supplied the people of Marlow, Lempster, Langdon, and elsewhere, with grain, and established, at an early period, a custom, most honorably kept up in the direct line of the family succeeding to the homestead, of maintaining a moderate and uniform price for corn, at periods when scarcity tempted the cupidity of other owners. When the settlements on the other side of the river began, grateful tradition keeps the memory green of his services to the early pioneers toward a still newer and ruder frontier. But whether this was in any case before he abandoned the fort for his new dwelling-house in 1762, I do not undertake to say.

After 1761, it is very plain that things began rapidly to mend. Courage and confidence were restored by the five or six years of safety, though not of conscious security, which had been experienced; and settlers began slowly to come into the town. No doubt, Colonel Bellows was very active in bringing them here. We have seen that the General Court extended the privileges of the charter in 1761, for another year, and so on; and the town records show that an amount of business was done this year at the town meetings, indicative of life and hope and enterprise. As many as eight different men were found to take office; among other offices that of tything-man was filled by Lemuel Hatch. But, above all, provision was made for public worship—each settler being taxed seven shillings sterling, to pay for preaching, and a vote being passed to meet at the fort, or *near by*, on Lord's day. It is evident that the shadow of the fort was still deemed essential to full security. It was voted at this same meeting that Benjamin Bellows provide seats and other conveniences for said purpose. There is a record of three different town meetings held this year, indicating the activity of the town, and giving special proof of the solicitude to establish Divine worship. The first minister, the Rev. Mr. Jonathan Leavitt, was called and ordained before any meeting-house existed; and Mr. Israel Calkins was voted and paid "two dollars for his services in going for the ministers to attend Mr. Jonathan Leavitt's ordination." In 1762, the year in which Colonel Bellows built his own house, the fifth article in the warrant for the town meeting is, "to agree and provide some house for to meet in on Lord's day for the present year;" and, in the ensuing town-meeting, it was voted fifteenthly, (for town warrants had got to be as long as old-fashioned sermons by this time,) "that each settler or inhabitant work four days each, or pay twelve shillings toward setting up a frame for a meeting-house, fifty-six feet in length, and forty-two in breadth, and that *Benjamin Bellows make up the rest.*" It is plain enough that Benjamin Bellows is a sort of Uncle Sam, whom no body thinks it necessary to spare, and who winks benevolently at the pickings and stealings of his civic nephews.

This meeting-house, thus early commenced, was pitched on what is generally called "Uncle Si's Hill," all that existed of a village then, and for several years after, lying, I suppose, the other side of that rise of ground. The Colonel doubtless intended the town to centre about his homestead. The minister's lot was, I infer, where Parson Fessenden's house afterward stood, nearly opposite the north-eastern corner of the burial-ground. Parson Leavitt had an ominous name, and was not permitted to stay long with his small but generous congregation. The terms of his settlement in 1761 had been very liberal. Seventy-five pounds sterling were voted as a settlement, (for the word settlement was originally used of the endowment accompanying the placing of ministers, in the sense in which it is still used of marriage portions;) "£37 10*s*. for the first year, to rise annually £3 15*s*. until it amounts to £60; there to stand until there be eighty polls; then rise fifteen shillings per poll until it amount to £75; and there stand so long as he should continue pastor of the town." To this was added, of course, the ministerial lot, reserved for the first settled minister. Benjamin Bellows was to make up whatever the town could not, toward Mr. Leavitt's settlement and support.

What the exact cause of Mr. Leavitt's leaving was, does not appear. But it is handed down, that, having dragged home a negro slave, a woman, who had run away, by a rope attached to his saddle, Colonel Bellows declared that such cruelty should not be submitted to; that he had settled Parson Leavitt, and now he would unsettle him. Ministers, however, were not got rid of so easily in those days. Being settled for life, they had rights which they well understood; and it is plain that some considerable diplomacy was required to shake Mr. Leavitt off. A mutual council was agreed on, to be held the 19th of June, 1764; but, on May 17th, after a conference with a committee, of which Colonel Bellows was chairman, Mr. Leavitt discharged the town of all obligations, and retired, upon the payment of a certain sum; so that the council was never held. I have Mr. Leavitt's receipt from Colonel Bellows, of the money voted for his settlement and first year's salary.

The building of the first meeting-house seems to have been a very laborious undertaking. The town records are full of votes on the subject, of taxes laid, and labor and pains taken, to get it along. But, after all, it was never finished. The truth is, the laying out of roads, and the clearing of the forest, were more pressing matters. It was begun when only a handful of people existed in the town, more from a sense of public propriety, than of actual necessity; and before it could be completed—that is, about twenty years from its commencement—it was deemed more expedient to build a new house, on a far larger scale, than to complete the old one.

The Rev. Mr. Fessenden was settled in 1767, and soon after Mr. Leavitt's departure, showing the spirit and energy of the town. His settlement was placed upon a still more liberal basis than Mr. Leavitt's—his salary being fixed at fifty pounds the first year. He objected, very properly, to receiving more than "half his salary in wheat, at 4*s.* per bushel; rye, 3*s.* and Indian corn, 2*s.*; good beef, at 2 pence per pound, and good pork, at 3 pence; the pork being hoggs that weigh 8 score;" as it would compel him to turn merchant, and divert him from his proper duties—a remonstrance which the parish had the good sense to heed. In March, 1768, the town voted to have three schools in town for the winter season, and, in 1771, laid, in addition to the school tax, a further one to build schoolhouses; and every year, about this time, shows an increasing readiness and ability to support schools. In 1775, at the very time the town is patriotically voting to pay its "proportion of charge for the meeting of the Provincial Congress," it is also voting "to look a lot of land in Walpole for the use of a grammar-school, and to transact the affair with Colonel Bellows, and make report at the next meeting." The same year, at another town meeting, the town vote their "thanks to Colonel Benjamin Bellows for his generous gift of a lott of a hundred acres of land in the town of Walpole, for the use of a grammar-school in said town forever." It would be instructive to me, to learn what had become of said one hundred-acre lot, and where the grammar-school on said foundation forever is.

Thus, Colonel Bellows lived to see the great institutions of civilization established beyond any accident in the town he had founded. The church and the schoolhouse had been among his first cares, when the withdrawal of the savages and the coming in of settlers gave him an opportunity of promoting them, and his descendants have only been called on to sustain what he had the more difficult task of founding in a wilderness. The impression of him I receive, both from the town records and the traditions of the neighborhood, is, that he possessed an extraordinary resolution, energy, and activity of character, and shrunk from no amount of care, and from no kind of service essential to the accomplishment of his objects, as the founder of a town. Mr. Lyman Watkins remembers hearing one of the older members of his own family say, that Nathan Watkins, the first settler of the Watkins' race in Walpole, who was a batteauxman on the Mohawk, stopped here on his way home to Ashford, Connecticut, and was beset and induced by Colonel Bellows to remain. Repenting, however, of his purpose, he concluded to leave, but was pursued by the Colonel, the moment he heard of his departure, overtaken at Westmoreland, and coaxed back to Walpole. He remembered that the horse, on which the very large body of the Colonel was mounted, was black, and seemed small under its rider, and that the determination of the Colonel was of a very irresistible character. This is, probably, only a sample of his usual energy and success in procuring and retaining settlers. The times required great presence of mind, and great bodily courage. The Colonel had both. It is related of him, that, on a certain occasion, he went up on Fall Mountain alone, and, though not on the look-out for large game, came upon a full-grown bear, which he managed to shoot. Shortly after, another Bruin appeared, and met the same fate from the Colonel's gun, who began, however, to think his black customers too thick and ugly. Hardly had he disposed of his second victim, when he heard a loud rustling in the bushes near, and, looking over his shoulder, beheld a pair of glaring eye-balls fixed upon him from above the brakes. The Colonel knew at once that he had a different adversary to deal with here from the clumsy bear, and that his best hope of escape lay in killing outright the beast, which, merely wounded, might prove too much for him. Though an excellent shot, he raised his gun with no little trepidation, and aimed straight at the eyes. No bound of the animal followed his fire, and not liking to investigate too curiously a path lined with such vermin, he beat a rapid retreat. Returning shortly with his men, he carried home two large bears—a delicious meat, so esteemed—and an enormous catamount, measuring a fabulous number of feet from the tip of his nose to the tip of his tail. The catamount was very much dreaded by all the best New-England hunters, and it was considered very imprudent for a single hunter to attack one. A Mr. Chase, of Gilmanton, who chanced to kill one single-handed, went ever after by the *soubriquet* of Catamount Chase.

He manifested, very obviously, great discretion as a founder, alike in the public spirit and liberality of his own doings, and in the modesty and unobtrusiveness of his conduct. There was nothing to overshadow or wound the pride and independence of the early settlers, in his bearing toward them. He showed, indeed, the same kind of disposition to throw off upon others, as soon as any persons could be found to bear them, the honors and dignities of the town, as he did to make his children, at the earliest moment, independent of him, in respect of worldly goods. There was no selfishness, no mean economy, no backwardness to share his power or place, while there was no ostentation of benevolence, no bustling assertion of paternal authority, no claim to absorb the influence or control of the town.

He was a man of a good English education for the times, possessing the accomplishments of a legible hand-writing and an intelligible spelling. I suspect his early life threw him much into what is called good society, the society of men of education and manners. The country, at that period, contained many persons connected with the army or the government, besides agents for English owners or speculators, who brought the manners and the education of the old country with them. Colonel Bellows, through his brothers-in-law, Rev. Mr. Stearns and Colonel Blanchard; through the family of his mother, the Willards; and by his connection, as a surveyor and purveyor for the army, with the English officers, had probably formed manners of considerable dignity, and of more courtesy and authority than is usual among farmers in the more democratic rule of our day. He had, in short, seen more of the world. Some of his children, more especially the General and Colonel John, were distinguished for a suavity and courtliness of manner, a carefulness and nicety of dress, indicative of hereditary refinement.

It was not a day of books or schools; and judging from the scarcity of Colonel Bellows's correspondence, and from the general character of his descendants, it is probable that the great books of nature and of man formed his principal library. His descendants have uniformly been more distinguished for native shrewdness, than for cultivated power—for the faculty of influencing their fellow-beings by sympathy or insight, than for skill in argument and demonstration. Of educated Bellows's, there are, fortunately, now a great many; but I know of no one who has shown a decided passion for learning. There is now at least no ground for the old slur cast by some one of the wits of Joe Denny's time upon the race, that "If you put a Bellows into a room with a book, and he could get out no other way, he would jump from the window." Still, it is creditable to the mental constitution of the family, that its hereditary bias is toward intercourse with human beings rather than books; that it seeks its knowledge at first sight, by observation, and not at second-hand, by reading; and this strong trait I suppose to be an honest inheritance from the old Colonel. He was an eminently practical person, living by deeds and not by words. It is related of him, that his knowledge of the woods and trees on the one hand, and of the art of building on the other, was so great, that he would go into the forest with his men, and point out at once in the standing trees such as were suited to each special timber in the barn—these for plates, those for rafters, such for posts, and such others for cross-ties—and that his energy and power of business were so grand, that, in the case of new settlers, whom he wished to encourage and fasten to the soil, he would sometimes build a barn in a day, cutting down the timber in the morning, and framing and raising the structure before night—a great story, but vouched for by ancient and excellent living authority.

Colonel Bellows died July 10th, 1777. He had lived since the year 1762 in the large and (for the times) exceedingly well-built and well-finished house inherited by his son Thomas. The carpentry and finish of that and other houses built before his death in Walpole, show that the mechanics of those days were masters of their trade, and had the English thoroughness and patience, and the English model of building before their eyes. It took, as I have heard, an incredible time to finish some of these wainscotted houses, and must have consumed no small amount of money. Colonel Bellows lived in a style of large hospitality. All strangers, travellers, and public men stopped at his house; and such was the number of hands his immense landed estate compelled him to employ, that his household had a patriarchal character. A very large kitchen under the house, where a great oaken table lay always spread, was the eating-room of his workmen. He always maintained a separate table for his immediate family, saying, that next to religion itself, he held family ties sacred, and did not wish to have the sanctity of the fire-side and the domestic board invaded by outsiders. The Colonel raised his own stores, and killed an ox or a cow every week to supply the wants of his household. The winter stores were enormous in quantity, and the annual consumption fearful to contemplate in these days of comparative scarcity. The Colonel put down twenty barrels of pork yearly; eggs were brought in by the half-bushel; and his men stipulated that they should not have *salmon* oftener than three times a week. He made four hundred barrels of cider per annum. He had married for his second wife, at Lunenberg, in April, 1758, the widow Jennison, whose maiden name was Mary Hubbard.* Their children were Abigail, Theodore, Thomas, Mary, Josiah, all born between 1759 and 1767, so that at the time of his death he had nine children living, the youngest being ten years old.

Colonel Bellows manifested a lively interest in public religion, as we have seen; he also showed his interest in religion as a private concern, both by the practical respect in which he held its precepts, and by maintaining in his own family a minister, who acted as chaplain. Rev. Elisha Harding, a graduate of Harvard, was settled at West-Brookfield, Mass., and left his parish, it is now said, on account of some affair of the heart, a difficulty to which ministers seem to have the same exposure as other men. He came to Walpole early, and lived in Colonel Bellows's family until the time of his employer's death, when he removed into the General's household, and died there in 1794. His grave-stone is found in our burial-ground, and two children of Colonel Caleb Bellows lie on either side of his grave, as if their father had sought to place them in death under the protection of the good man's dust, whose voice had led the prayers of his own father's house.

I can not possibly give a more graphic account of the manners of the time, than to quote entire from the *Cheshire Gazette*, of April 28, 1826, a paper understood to be prepared by our respected townsman, Dr. Morse, from a communication made to him, in consequence of his papers touching the Indians in Walpole, from which I have already drawn largely.

A Mrs. Watson, of Germantown, Pa., was alive in 1826,

* Parson Stearns, of Lunenberg, had also married a sister of this lady, whose maiden name was Hubbard. The family were from Townsend, Mass. Colonel John Bellows also married a Hubbard, a niece of his father's second wife, and sister to Professor John Hubbard, of Hanover College.

who resided in Walpole in 1762, then only eight years old, but whose power of memory seemed wonderfully precise.

"It seems"—thus the story begins—"that a Mr. John Fanning, the father of the narrator, left Stonington, Conn., with a view of establishing himself on Otter Creek, Vt., but, owing to the difficulties of travelling in new countries, advanced no further than Walpole. In 1762, the family took passage in a sloop of their own as far as Hartford, where they purchased a wagon and two horses, to convey them up the east side of the river. The country, as far as Chicopee river, is represented as remarkably fine, both as respects the fertility of the soil and the improvements of the settlers. Hatfield was then a small town, having been recently destroyed by the Indians. This calamity is said to have been forewarned by some of the inhabitants having, as they supposed, heard a few nights previous, the approach of tribes of savages, and the sound of their snow-shoes. The fields of grain were immense, without any division fences. At Sunderland, the road then travelled was mountainous, which rendered it necessary to leave some of their articles, and purchase a yoke of oxen to help them along. They next passed a small village called Keene, and came to Walpole, No 3. (? When was the first road laid out from Walpole to Keene; was it before a river-road was made ?) There they purchased a lot of land, (now (1826) the Philips' farm,) built a house of square timber, cut down the trees and cleared the land, so as to raise a good crop of corn the same year. The roof of the house was covered with bark, and the gable ends remained open some time, which enabled them to hear the barking of foxes, the howling of wolves, and the cries of the panther, while sitting before the fire. The latter resembled the voice of a woman in distress, and (seemed) intended to decoy people into the woods, where the salutations of these raving gentry were apt to prove troublesome, unless prevented by the presence of fire-arms. The flesh of the deer and the bear afforded the settlers many a delicious repast; the approach of the latter was often unceremonious, and sometimes rude to strangers. Wild turkeys were trapped and shot, and quails and pigeons caught in nets in great abundance. The brooks were filled with trout and dace, and the river abounded in salmon and shad; one of the latter was taken near the falls which had a rattle-snake's head in its stomach. An intercourse with the animal creation was carried to an unusual length. A brood of young raccoons were taught to suck the cat, and play about the house like kittens, only much more mischievous. The effect of this wild mode of living was exemplified in the case of a Mrs. Prichard, who was lost in the woods, and subsisted, like wild beasts, on berries and bark of trees twenty-one days. She started, during a thunder-shower, from a place called Jennison's Hill, to visit a neighbor's house, with a child of two years old. Leaving the track to avoid a large snake, she lost her way, and was not seen again till just three weeks, when some men discovered her near the mouth of Cold River. She fled at the sight of men like a deer, but was overtaken and brought back to a house. Her clothes were completely torn off. After recovering her senses in a degree, she stated that her child died the third day, which she buried under a log. She said she heard the Indians' guns, and saw them several times in pursuit of her, (probably her friends, who spent several days looking for her,) but she secreted herself so as to elude their vigilance. She was living in Westminster a few years ago in a state of mental alienation.

"The country was pretty much cleared of Indians, but the hardships of the primitive settlers, and their frequent rencontres with wild beasts and savages, furnished a fruitful topic of conversation, with which to spend the evening, and regale their distant friends who visited them.

"A man by the name of Root, was delightfully serenaded all night by a bear and two cubs at the foot of a tree, while he lodged on the limbs above.

"A Mrs. Wheeler, of Keene, was one of seven women who bravely defended a fort, without any other weapons than *boiling soap*. The men were gone into the woods with all the guns, when the Indians made their attack. By keeping up a well-directed fire of that hot article in the face and eyes of the assailants, as they approached the port-holes, the women finally succeeded in routing the enemy.

"At this time, 1762, there were about twelve or fifteen log-houses in the town. The meeting-house was unfinished; there was not a carriage in town; the travelling being performed on foot or horseback; sometimes three or four children were carried in this way at a time, beside a wife on the pillion, and upsetting a load of this magnitude was not an uncommon occurrence.

"Colonel B. Bellows was the most considerable man in the town; his eldest son, Peter, was settled in Charlestown, where the people used often to go to attend meeting. A remarkable trait in the character of the first settlers was their punctuality in attending public worship. Mr. Leavitt, the minister, like other clergymen of that day, wore a large wig, full-powdered, and when he entered the meeting-house, the whole congregation rose to do obeisance to the man in black, who, in his turn, always responded with a formal bow. Powder was not worn on the hair by those who were contented with the use of the eel-skin, which was considered as adding dignity to the wearer, in proportion to the size and length of the *queue*. Officers of the militia wore cocked hats. Of the ladies, Mrs. Leavitt took the lead in dress; at church she wore a full suit of brocade lutestring, without any bonnet, holding a fan to shade the sun from her face, as was the fashion 'down country.'

"Next to her were the daughters of Colonel Bellows, and their two half-sisters, Jenisons. They wore plain, Quaker bonnets of black silk; white or colored ones were not seen. To improve their figures, the ladies quilted their petticoats with wool, to make their hips show off to advantage, which contrasted with the smallness of the waist, painfully compressed with long stays. Home-made durants, camblets, and serges, full of gay flowers of artificial needlework, were fashionable articles. Stockings, of their own knitting, and high-heeled shoes with buckles, were indispensable. It was thought an improvement to beauty and elegance to expose the petticoat before, through a screen or lawn apron, the gown being left to swing open. The hair was all combed back, leaving no curls or ringlets about the face. Instead of following the modern fashion of covering the *back* part of the head, their bonnets were so much pitched forward, that the cap and back part of the head were exposed.

"A large portion of *pin-money* was derived from the sale of golden thread, ginseng, and snake-root, which were procured from their own hands.

"Doctor Chase was the only physician."

The article from which this interesting communication is taken closes with the words "to be continued;" but we have not been able to find the conclusion, and suspect it was never published. Bating a few anachronisms, and a little confusion of recollection, we doubt not it gives an accurate picture of the manners of the time.

I can not conclude my account of Colonel Bellows without saying, that he appears to have been a man of humane feelings and tender domestic affections. If any characteristics belong to his descendants, I should say they were a hatred of cruelty, a strong natural sympathy with suffering, and a stable attachment to their own blood and the home of the family. We probably owe much of these traits to our common ancestor. I have already remarked upon the liberality with which the old Colonel settled his children about him as early in life as they could possibly be brought forward. When his son Joseph, who was settled in Lunenberg, came occasionally to Walpole with his family, the whole race was put in motion. The father and all the sons' households joined in going the rounds of the family in honor of the visitor, and they extended their visits in company even to Peter's house in Charlestown. Thus wisely did the old patriarch lay the foundations of family union among his children, and they have not lost the lesson, our family being, on the whole, quite remarkable for the absence of domestic feuds, and the existence of united and affectionate feelings. The remarkable disposition manifested to return and die in the old family home—a disposition which is gathering more and more of the children of our race near the ashes of their ancestor, is a proof how strong is the family affection, and how deep a place our founder hollowed out for it here in our native valley. His monument, overlooking from its marble height the village of our love, will never, I believe, look upon fewer of his descendants' roofs, in the landscape it commands, than now. Our children will not love

Walpole less, because still more of their fathers' dust has mingled with its soil.

In person, Col. Benjamin Bellows was tall and stout, not to say immense. His weight, at or near the time of his decease, was three hundred and thirty pounds. It is no small proof of the extraordinary energy of his spirit, that, until within the few last years of his life, this bulk did not encumber his movements nor repress his activity. Mounted on a strong sorrel horse,* able to carry him and his youngest son, Josiah, who rode behind, and slipped off readily to take down the bars in his visits to his various fields, Col. Bellows rode about his farm and directed the labor of his men. From him descended, perhaps, our characteristic love of horses; and from him came the Herculean frames which the next generation possessed, unhappily not perpetuated beyond it. It is said, that of all his grandchildren or descendants, the late Col. Seth Hunt, of this town, most resembled him in appearance.† A man of great amiability and true benevolence, with a natural suavity and courtliness of manner that procured for him the title of one of nature's gentlemen; honest as he was energetic, rare in judgment, of great self-possession under trying emergencies, strong in body and mind, unbounded in hospitality, and sagacious and prophetic in plans, the old Colonel united the qualities of his well-known sons, the General and Colonel John, and was the large and pure fountain of his numerous and decided race. Blessings on his memory!

Leaving now the old Founder, I turn to his children, in the expectation, however, of merely sketching their characters and history, without much regard either to chronology or completeness. And here let me beg my kinsmen to throw their sensitiveness aside and allow me to tell the simple truth. I can not, for the gratification of the affections or pride of any

* One of a span which he sometimes drove in a curricle, the first and only carriage, it must have been, of the time; for, according to Mr. Hale, as late as 1792 there was only one vehicle or carriage known to be kept and used in Keene for pleasure travelling. It was not till later that Judge Newcomb introduced the first chaise. No stage at that time (1792) had ever passed through the streets.

† Uncle Ben, Joseph's son, still living, and the only one of his descendants who remembers the old Colonel, does not indorse this opinion. He describes his bulkiness as prodigious, and thinks his shoes were wholly cut off from his own view by a rotundity of vast exuberance. The favorite chair, which indicates his grand proportions, is now in possession of his grandson, Abel Bellows, Esq.

branch of the family, assign virtues which did not exist, or wholly cover faults which were prominent, in any of our several ancestors. My feeling is, that we each have a claim in the virtues of the whole family, and a responsibility for the faults of the whole. Taking Col. Bellows's family altogether, it was a most worthy and excellent family, one we may be proud to have sprung from; and although that one of his sons from which I derive my honored father's father, was smitten by the hand of God with insanity, and able to do little for the dignity and reputation of the race, yet I do not the less feel like perpetuating the names and memory of his more prosperous and distinguished brothers.

The oldest son, as we have seen, was Peter. He was a man of small stature, who married into the highly respectable family of the Chases, and lived at Charlestown. Perhaps it was no special advantage to him that he was the eldest son of a father reputed rich, and indulgent; and he seems to have been somewhat less disposed to exertion than the other sons, with the exception of Theodore, who bore among the younger set of children somewhat Peter's place among the older set. A good deal has been said to me of Peter's bravery. I find that at a very tender age he was made constable of the town; and it appears that he went to Ticonderoga in June 28, 1777, just a fortnight before his father's death, as a private in Col. Walker's company.

At the close of the celebrated Kilburn's fight, which ended in the evening, the occupants of Colonel Bellows's fort were in a state of great anxiety as to the result, not knowing whether the Indians had been successful or had retired, but fearing that Kilburn and his family had been killed. The anxiety of uncle Peter was so great, that he determined to ascertain their fate if possible, and for that purpose he left the fort late in the evening, and alone, to pass through what was then an unbroken wilderness, and filled, as might reasonably be supposed, with Indians. He crept through, using all the caution of a hunter, and at length arrived safely at Kilburn's house; and having carefully reconnoitred and ascertained that it was still held by Kilburn, he asked and obtained admittance, and was the first to congratulate him upon his successful defense.

He was distinguished for wit as well as courage, and

could furnish very good company to any body disposed to a merry time. I have heard that he was famous for the point and readiness of his repartees, which he could even put into very good rhyme at short notice; and among these witticisms was his own epitaph, which is described to me as exceedingly funny and smart, but I have not been able to recover it. Peter had a good many children, but his race did not thrive in health, and many of its members died early. His living at Charlestown separated him more than was desirable from the family, who have known less of his race than they ought. He has left many highly respectable descendants.

Benjamin Bellows, known so long during his life and now remembered as *the General*, was the second son of his father, having been born October 6th, 1740. He married Phœbe Strong, sister of Governor Strong, of Northampton; had five children, and died June, 1802. As he was undoubtedly the most distinguished member of his family, and very particularly connected with public affairs, I must devote a much larger space to him than to any other of the old Colonel's children.

The General came forward very early in life. He was made town-clerk (in 1759) when only nineteen years of age, and held the office thirty-six years. His early education, carried on with that of his other brothers, at Northampton, (where, by a pleasant coïncidence, the writer had the advantage of passing four years of his own preparatory schooling,) must have been very good; for the town records show that he wrote an elegant hand from an early period, and commanded a correct and fluent style. Being constitutionally of a mild and winning temperament, and having an old head on young shoulders, he was clearly strong in the confidence of his father and of the town, from very early manhood. He held in succession every office of trust and dignity which the town or the county could confer, and almost every honor and position within the gift of the State. He was alike active in civil and in military affairs, and the times demanded efficiency in both; being a prompt and competent officer, both in command of his regiment or brigade, and in the management of the military chest of the State, of which he was a trusted and efficient agent; while he still more distinguished himself in what better suited his taste and temperament, the conduct of legislative and municipal concerns.

Clerk, treasurer, selectman, road-surveyor, no office was so humble or so laborious that he despised or shrunk from its duties in the affairs of the town; Register of Deeds for many years, member and usually chairman of every committee called on county business; principal adviser and director, so far as the towns on this side the line were concerned, in all the great boundary question between Vermont, New-Hampshire, New-York, and Massachusetts; member of the General Court, under the first Governor of the State; first senator, and next counsellor, in 1777 and in 1781, he attained every distinction except that of Governor, an office to which he was once nominated, and which he would admirably have filled.

Perhaps his principal official distinction in civil life was in being chosen President of the College of Electors in this State, for the choice of the first President of the United States, January 7th, 1789. He was also Elector of President when John Adams was chosen. His temper admirably fitted him for legislative duties, he being of a fair and balanced mind, of great natural candor, and perfect self-control, with a punctilious conscientiousness fortified by warm religious feelings, and an urbane and dignified presence, which commanded confidence and respect.

Whiton, in his Sketches of the History of New-Hampshire, from its settlement in 1623 to 1833, says, on page 151:

"Among those who were distinguished patriots of the Revolution, and had influence in the public counsels of the State, are, in addition to the names of President Weare and John Langdon, those of John Pickering and Woodbury Langdon, of Portsmouth; Nathaniel Peabody, of Atherton; Nicholas Gilman, John T. Gilman, and Nathaniel Folsom, of Exeter; Geo. Frost and Eben Thompson, of Durham; John Dudley, of Raymond; Sam Lawrence, of Holdman; Josiah Bartlett, of Kingston; Timothy Walker, of Concord; John McClary, of Epsom; Matthew Thornton, of Merrimac; Jonathan Blanchard, of Dunstable; Wiseman Claggett, of Litchfield; Matthew Patten, of Bedford; and Benjamin Bellows, of Walpole."

The same author says, (page 158:)

"The convention elected in New-Hampshire to decide the great question of ratifying or rejecting the Federal Constitution, met at Exeter, in February, 1788. They appointed General Sullivan to be their President, and the Hon. John Calfe their Secretary. This respectable body included most of the eminent men of the State. In the list of its members are found the names of Langdon, Pickering, Bartlett, John T. Gilman, Atherton, Parker, Bellows, West, Livermore, and Badger."

Turning to his military services, we must recollect that he lived before and through the period of the Revolutionary War; that he rose from the lowest office in the militia of the State to be a Brigadier-General, through his actual services to the State and country. Although not in the field for a very considerable portion of the time, he was largely engaged in raising troops for the regular United States service, and was counted on by the General and the State Government as a dependable, prompt, and efficient man, whenever any military steps were to be taken.

Twice he marched his own regiment to Ticonderoga, first in October 1776, for a service of twenty-five days; and again, June 28th, 1777, to reïnforce the garrison there when besieged by the enemy, when, according to the pay-roll, the time of service was only twelve days. Finally, he carried his regiment, September 21st, 1777, to reïnforce the Northern Continental army at Saratoga, under the command of Gen. Gates, at the time when Burgoyne surrendered.

The historian says, after a battle "severe and bloody," the "victory of the Americans was complete." General Gates detached strong bodies of his troops in various directions, to cut off the retreat of the enemy. Burgoyne retired by Saratoga Creek to the Hudson, at which point he was met by the New-Hampshire militia, under the command of Colonels Webster, Bellows, and Morey. At this place the enemy halted, and Burgoyne observed that "it was vain to contend with the owners of the soil." Therefore he and his army laid down their arms, and surrendered themselves prisoners of war.*

In his account with the government is a charge for a horse killed in his service, but whether killed under the Colonel or not I cannot say.

Mr. Lyman Watkins reports that some of the old soldiers from Walpole, who went with the General, used to say that the regiment captured one hundred and fifty Indians the first day of their service. Among the Walpole men in that battle were Crane and Hall, who went out as scouts, and fell in with Indians. Crane had a dreadful encounter with an Indian armed with a cutlass, which, in the struggle, he grasped, cutting his fingers in such a way as to be unable to open

* Vol. 3, Hist. Coll., p. 274.

his hand ever after. Munn Hall, of Walpole, is reported to have said to Burgoyne at the surrender, "We've got you for breakfast, and we 'll have Lord Cornwallis for dinner."

All the able-bodied men in town went to Saratoga. The Squire remembered the names of twelve, among which were Ephraim Stearns, Farnham, Messer, Lawrence, Massey, etc.; and it is a somewhat characteristic anecdote of the Sheriff, that when telling over the list, and not being able to recall the twelfth man, he added, "No matter, 't was a black man any way." This black man was also a blacksmith, who had his shop on a farm near the meeting-house, now owned by Henry J. Watkins.

The General claimed to have seen some Indian service, and used to wear, on high military occasions, a belt of wampum, as a trophy of victory over the savages. Several Walpole men brought other trophies from this battle. The father of J. H. Wire had some harnesses, a powder-chest, and hatchet, which could be seen a few years since. One of the Kilburns, with some men, captured a boat belonging to the enemy, which contained a keg they fancied must be rum. They bored into it with their bayonets, and found it *pork*. The authority does not say whether or no they were disappointed.

General Gates highly complimented the regiments from Cheshire county, under Col. Ashley and Col. Bellows, for their services on this occasion. His letter runs thus:

"TICONDEROGA, Nov. 9, 1776.

"GENTLEMEN: I return you and the officers and soldiers of the regiments under your command, my thanks for the spirit and expedition both you and they have shown in marching, upon the first alarm, upwards of one hundred miles, to the support of this important pass, when threatened with an immediate attack from the enemy's army. I now dismiss you with the honor you have so well deserved. I further certify that neither you nor any under your command have received any pay or reward from me, for your services on this occasion; *that* I leave to be settled by the General Congress with the convention of your State.

"With great respect, I am, gentlemen,

"Your most obedient, humble servant,

"HORATIO GATES.

"To Col. ASHLEY and Col. BELLOWS, Commanders the Regiments of Militia from the County of Cheshire, in the State of New-Hampshire."

Whenever men were to be raised for the war, in any part

of the North, New-Hampshire, and Cheshire and Walpole were always ready; and Gen. Bellows was the agent through whom all recruits and all payments were made. The army-rolls are full of his activity.

Perhaps, however, the best military service he ever rendered was nearer home, namely, at Westminster, on the 14th March, 1775, when he was a simple captain. Fully to understand the value of his services, more explanation than the time allows would be required. The new generations have little conception of the violent internal controversies that rent our young life as a nation, at the very time we needed all our energy to contend with foreign invasion. Perhaps in bitterness, the quarrel between Vermont, then called the New-Hampshire grants, from being composed of lands granted by our New-Hampshire provincial Governor and Council—and New-York, then a province, took precedence of all others, and afterwards gave the General Government most uneasiness. New-York claimed jurisdiction over the whole territory now called Vermont, under the charter of Charles II. "The New-Hampshire grants" resisted this jurisdiction, wishing, at first, to fall under the control of New-Hampshire, but afterwards to be wholly free and independent.

Some of the people of Vermont sympathized with the New-York or royal claim, and of course the country was filled with civil feuds. The owners of the lands who had bought and paid for them under the New-Hampshire grant, were of course not willing to confess the illegitimacy of the authority under which they held their titles; while New-York naturally relinquished very slowly the control of so fair and promising a district of country. After a great deal of exasperation and controversy, the people in Cumberland county determined that the New-York royal court should not be held at Westminster, at its approaching session, and accordingly, after peaceably attempting to dissuade the judges from holding the court, and obtaining some equivocal promises, they seized the court-house, (though without arms,) on the afternoon of the day when the court was to be holden. The royal authorities, determined not to be put down by a mob, prepared to enforce their rights by arms; and in the short struggle which ensued, William French, a young man twenty-two years of age, was shot in the court-house at eleven o'clock at night, and dragged by the enraged authorities, whose blood was now up, out of the house, with many oaths and indignities, and challenges to the people.* The Westminster folks, with their friends from neighboring towns, were terribly enraged at what they termed this massacre, and surrounded the court-house all night, in serious doubt whether or not to burn it down with the whole court in it, as a fitting sacrifice to their vengeance. General Bellows (then Captain) heard of the terrible excitement, hastened at the head of his company, to the ground, and mingling in the crowd, as the professed friend and aider of the popular cause against this royal oppression, soon so far got possession of the confidence of the mob as to convert their threatened lynch law to regular legal action. He persuaded the maddened people, who might otherwise have gone to the extremity of a general butchery of the royalists, to seize the principal men, and carry them, under his escort, to Northampton, where the only strong jail could be found, out of disputed territory. This was done; and although the interference of New-York procured afterwards the liberation of the prisoners, yet time was gained, and a bloody and most disastrous consummation averted. It has been said that the news of the massacre at Westminster, with its consequences, reaching General Gage at Boston, exasperated him, as an indication of the spirit of our people, to march to Lexington and inflict the blow which introduced the Revolutionary War and the Declaration of Independence. No event, at any rate in General Bellows's life, was more important or more honorable than his pacific influence at the Westminster massacre.

Gen. Bellows, and Col. John, his next brother, the moment

* Mr. French's epitaph still stands in the burial-ground at Westminster, and runs thus:

"In memory of WILLIAM FRENCH, son to Mr. Nathaniel French, who was shot at Westminster, March ye 13th, 1775, by the hands of cruel ministerial tools of Georg ye 3d, in the corthouse, at a 11 a clock at night, in the 22d year of his age.

Here William French his body lies.
For murder his blood for vengeance cries.
King Georg the third, his Tory crew,
Tha with a bawl his head shot threw.
For Liberty and his country's Good
He lost his Life, his Dearest blood."

From Slade's Vermont State Papers.

they heard of the battle of Lexington, 19th April, 1775, hasted towards the scene, followed by a party of volunteers. At Keene they found that Capt. Wyman, with thirty volunteers, had already gone. Riding to the house of Capt. Wyman, and learning that he started at sunrise, they exclaimed, "Keene has shown a noble spirit," and hastened onwards. Thirty-five volunteers from Walpole, it appears from the pay-roll, followed Capt. John Bellows to Lexington, who was absent eleven days on this expedition.

The town was not backward in manifesting its interest in the Revolution. The town record contains a set of most spirited instructions to Capt. Christopher Webber, sent as a representative to Exeter in 1776. It indicates some rising attention to literature and scholarship, that these instructions were received by the town from the committee appointed to draw them up, with this qualification, that is, "*With amend ments to make it grammar.*" In 1778, the town voted to take care of the families of the men engaged in the Continental service, and was always ready to meet the due demands on it for men or money, towards the common service.

Gen. Bellows took a very important part in the serious difficulties that arose about 1781, between New-Hampshire and Vermont, respecting the boundary. New-Hampshire, finding that New-York was making so large a claim on the territory of Vermont, then known as the New-Hampshire grants, determinded to claim jurisdiction herself over such of the river towns as chose to put themselves under her government. Gen. Bellows was Chairman of a Convention, held in Walpole, 15th Nov., 1780, of Delegates from Cumberland, Gloster, and Grafton counties, Vermont, and of towns on this side the Connecticut River, in which it was resolved to hold a more general meeting to consolidate a union of the grants. The meeting blames New-Hampshire for her want of spirit in not pushing her claims west of the river. In January, 1781, a Convention, which delegates from forty-three towns attended, met at Charlestown, and confirmed the resolution to claim jurisdiction over such portions of the New-Hampshire grants as chose to acknowledge New-Hampshire as their government. The Vermont Legislature, indignant at this, retaliated by claiming jurisdiction on the east side of the river, and some how found means to decoy sixteen towns into a desertion of New-Hampshire for Vermont. As the matter ripened, Walpole itself, among thirty-four other towns in the western portion of this State, was in favor of union with Vermont. It is probable that the western portion of New-Hampshire felt some jealousy of the eastern portion, and, not without reason, judged that a union of the river towns on both sides would be for the common benefit of a new State, to be called New-Connecticut. At any rate, the majority of the people in this town was in favor of such a union, and Vermont, nothing loth, begun to hold her Courts in Charlestown and Chesterfield, and to dispute the rights of New-Hampshire to a peaceful jurisdiction there. Gen. Bellows, who knew the whole State, and was loyal to it all, could not look on this dismemberment without indignation and alarm; and I find several able and earnest letters of his, addressed to the first Governor, Mr. Weare, setting forth in very cogent and somewhat wrathful language the audacity of the Vermont authorities, and the necessity of prompt, efficient, and decisive resistance. He says that he already has concealed in his house two officers of New-Hampshire, who would be torn in pieces if they should fall into the hands of the supporters of the Vermont jurisdiction. He counsels the Governor to strengthen the enfeebled powers of the Sheriff of Cheshire with the *posse comitatus* of the State, and gives it as his opinion that the seizure and confinement of the ringleaders would terrify and suppress the mob. These letters are full of judgment, of mingled energy and moderation, and show the General to have been both a skillful diplomatist and a resolute and loyal man, not disposed to yield to mere majorities (for the town was on the other side) when matters of right and public duty were concerned. Happily, the turn of affairs soon came to the support and victory of the General's counsel. The west bank of the Connecticut was settled, with Washington's advice, as the eastern line of Vermont, and Walpole, a little against her will, continued in the old Granite State, retaining her own seal in place of the *beech seal*, the Vermont symbol under the Counsel of Safety, who applied a beechen club to the backs of all the New-York invaders of her territory, as her mark of state.

I could very much extend my history of the General's

public services, and illustrate, by the aid of them, the history of the town and county, but I must hasten to more personal matters.

General Bellows was distinguished for the purity and excellence of his life and character, for the dignity and courtesy of his manners, for his natural powers of persuasion and command.

His civic and military spirit and services did not swallow up his domestic and personal virtues and usefulness. He was early elected a Deacon of the church, but declined the office, probably from some sense of military propriety. He was appointed, I find, by the church books, to read the Psalm in public worship, as being, probably, the gravest and most dignified member of the congregation. When the new church was built on the hill, he testified his interest in the institutions of religion by buying fourteen out of the eighty-eight pews in the house. He adopted his father's chaplain into his family, old Elisha Harding, and when Deacon Foster, who had married the writer's great-grandmother, Mrs. Whitney, and became a member of Col. Joseph's family at Lunenburg, came to Walpole, on the removal of the family—after Joseph's misfortunes and insanity—the General, Mr. Harding being dead, received and maintained Deacon Foster until the time of his death. Family worship, and grace before and after meat were always practised in the General's family. The good old Deacon was distinguished for the excellence of his prayers, and had the warm affection of the General. He lies buried in our graveyard, though his ashes are not marked with any stone.*

The General practised, after his father's example, an extensive hospitality. His house was open to every body, his hand and purse as open to the cry of want; tenderness, sincerity, and goodness of heart seem to have been singularly blended in him with good judgment and business accuracy. He does not appear to have been a man of original and striking powers of mind; nothing of a philosopher, with no accomplishments or

* The good Deacon was a better man than poet. He once called on a lady, still living, whose parents had been distinguished for worth, and thus addressed her:

"Recount the noble actions of your blood;
And what in them thou hast seen great and good,
Let be your pattern, that the world may see
Mother and grandmother alive in thee;
For two piouser women I never see."

gifts of learning, a plain man in his natural endowments, but with a grace, dignity, and real kindness, which gave him an undisputed eminence in his own neighborhood. What he said was law in Walpole. If any disturbance existed at the public house, his appearance would usually terminate it without a word. He ordered the boys into meeting as they stood round the Church, with a kind of mild authority which was never disputed. "There comes the General!" was the signal for decency and order; and the thump of his cane would quickly silence any unseemly noise. He would allow no jugglers or mountebanks in town, ordering them off on his own responsibility. He had a lively interest in all the people of the village, making it a rule, the first thing in the morning, to call upon and inquire after the sick. He and his brother John were punctilious in their visits to each other, and always extended the civility of a fresh pipe, of which both kept a store in *the oven*, which in the General's house was made perhaps for the purpose, by the fire-side in the sitting-room. Seated on opposite sides of the hearth, these ancient worthies discussed the news of the times.

The General was a dark-complexioned man, full six feet high, and very straight. He carried himself with military erectness and natural grace. Capt. Humphrey, of Portsmouth, told Mr. Abel Bellows, that when in attendance at the seat of Government as Senator or Counsellor, there was always a rivalry among the different boarding-houses as to who should entertain the General, so much was his attractiveness valued, and so highly did he stand in the good graces of the ladies. He wore a cocked hat, small clothes, and a cane, and was always nicely and carefully dressed.

A few anecdotes will illustrate the General's character. On one occasion the purchaser of a farm brought the General his deed to be recorded. The seller coming in before the record was made, asked to take the deed,* which the General, not

* In Rev. Mr. Arnold's History of Alstead a very interesting story is found, which illustrates Gen. Bellows's tenderness of character.

"In 1770, Jacob Cady, two and a half years old, son of Isaac Cady, was one day missing. The region around was one vast wilderness, and thickly inhabited by beasts of prey. Jacob, peculiarly dear to his mother, left her one afternoon to go to his father, chopping in the woods at a little distance. But when the father returned home at night, the child was missing. The anxious parents flew immediately in search of their little boy, and the more they hunted and called as the thick dark-

suspecting evil, allowed, and the rascally fellow refused afterward to give it up. The poor purchaser had no remedy

ness of night gathered around them, the more their anxiety increased and their hopes desponded. The night was spent in anxious search and awful suspense. But all their care and toil were vain. The light of morning returned, and yet their child was lost. But the day was now before them, and parental affection does not easily relinquish its object. The neighbors, though distant and few, were friendly and kind. Some immediately joined with the afflicted parents in ranging the woods, and others carried information to the neighboring towns. But the day declined, and the hopes which were for a time enkindled sunk in despondency as the darkness closed upon the light. Fires were kindled at distances from each other, suited to direct their search and attract the attention of the child, and numbers spent the night in fruitless attempts for his recovery.

"As the light of another day gilded the horizon, and invited their renewed exertions, multitudes were collected from Charlestown, Walpole, Marlow, Keene, and all the neighboring towns, (400 or 500 persons in all,) to lend their assistance to make one united effort, and if possible to relieve the anxiety of these bereaved parents. Hope was again revived, and earnest expectations were entertained as the bands went forth to scour the woods, with critical and careful attention to every nook, and to every circumstance that might show signs of the lost child. In their faithful searches among the rocks, forest trees, and fallen timber, at one time they discovered the tracks of a child and those of a bear, or of some wild beast very near them. Eager and trembling were the pursuers. Soon, however, all indications of discovery disappeared, and as the day began to decline, they relinquished their object as hopeless, and many returned to the house of Mr. Cady. 'Alas!' said the mother, under the burthen of fatigue, a want of sleep, and a spirit sinking in despair, 'if I could know that the child was relieved from suffering, even by the devouring beasts, I could be still. Could I see a fragment of his torn limbs, I would say no more. But can I lie down to rest not knowing but my little Jacob is wandering and starving in yonder gloom? (The house overlooked two deep forests.) Can a fond parent forget her child or cease to look for the little wanderer? Even the sleep of night would be disturbed by the visionary dreams of his suffering state, and the seeming cries for a mother's aid.'

"Such artless eloquence as this could not fail to move those generous feelings and noble sentiments which our fathers inherited. It was sufficient to put in lively exercise that compassion and benevolence, that spirit of enterprise and perseverance, for which they were so much distinguished.

"Gen. Benjamin Bellows and Capt. Jennison of Walpole, Capt. John Burroughs of this town, Mr. Abner Bingham of Marlow, and a few others who had not left the house, immediately determined to renew the search. And even the prospect of approaching night only served to hasten their steps and nerve their weary limbs. They agreed on the following signal, and set off in the pursuit. If they should discover any signs of the child, *one gun* was to be discharged; if he should be found dead, or to have been destroyed, *two guns* were to be discharged; and if he should be found alive, the discharge of three would give notice. With anxious though enfeebled solicitude did the parents and those at the house listen to catch the first sound that might burst upon the ear from the still expanse of the south. No sooner had their eager attention begun to subside than the first signal was heard. Every countenance instantly glowed with a fluctuating crimson, which told the emotions of joy and fear that struggled alternately within. But these emotions soon gave way to a deadly paleness and fearful apprehensions when the second discharge was heard. Is the child dead? was the secret inquiry of every look. Now all were breathless to hear, and were afraid they should not. But soon the third discharge broke the dreadful suspense, and burst the veil of uncertainty that hung over the scene. The change that so quickly succeeded, the joy that kindled in every breast, glowed in every countenance, and sparkled in every eye, can be more easily imagined than described. The child was found asleep east or south-east of Warren's pond, and restored with peculiar satisfaction and joyful triumph to the embrace of its delighted parents by General Bellows of Walpole."

except against the General, who had no right to part with the deed. Some cunning friend advised the General that the grantee could not legally prove the delivery of the deed to him, as there was no witness present, provided the General would stoutly deny it. "What," said he, "tell a lie! God forbid I should tell a lie for a farm."

Again, passing through Rockingham with my uncle Benjamin, on his return from Charlestown, he found a poor man's only cow being sold at a sheriff's sale. He bid it off himself, and gave it back to the man, bidding him pay him when he was able.

Passing through Surry at the time of a military review, when all the horses were in use, he found the landlady of the inn where he stopped, sick, and no horse procurable to send to Keene for Dr. Frink, the Twichell of those days. Said the General, "Here, take my horse, I can't let the woman die," and waited upon his journey until the return of the messenger.

Such a man could not fail to be loved, even more than he was honored, and his death was the signal for wide-spread grief. People from the neighboring towns came in upon the sad tidings, and filled our streets. Such a funeral procession was never seen in the town. The last of the mourners had not yet left the neighborhood of the house, when the head of the procession had reached the distant burial-ground. He was the worthy son of a worthy father, and his descendants are doubly honored in so pure and noble a line of ancestors.

Colonel John Bellows, the next son of our Founder, was born Nov. 3, 1742; he married Rebecca Hubbard; had twelve children, and died in 1812.

The town records show him to have been a public-spirited, efficient, and trusted citizen, occupying many successive posts of honor and dignity. His career was in many respects like that of his brother, the General; to whom, as his elder, he deferred in some degree. He participated in the military life of the General, being major in his regiment when he marched to Ticonderoga; and as captain he went to Lexington, at the head of thirty-five volunteers, the moment the news of the conflict came to town. He was much engaged through the Revolution in mustering men into the service, and in buying provisions for the army. He was a member of the State

Congress in 1775 and 1776, and of the Constitutional Convention in 1781, and Senator of the State in 1786 and 1787. He was made a Justice of the Peace throughout the State, June, 1807.

While the General did, perhaps, more for the public relations of the town, the Colonel did more for its business activity and agricultural enterprise. He was a great farmer, carrying on his concerns with a broad, comprehensive sense of his own interests and the interests of the town. Evidently he grasped at affairs with no common talent and energy, striking out new paths of industry and new modes of enterprise. He gave employment to people far and near, in spinning up the immense quantity of wool he raised. His house had often the appearance of a hotel, or a fair, from the number of horses hitched to his door-posts, or the number of guests seen at his table. Farmers' wives from the neighboring towns would come in on horseback to the Colonel's, bringing back the yarn, and in quest of their load of wool for the coming winter's spinning. The horse was put up for the night, and the rider being comfortably lodged and refreshed, set off after breakfast the next morning, loaded with bags of wool, for the distant home.

Colonel John was the moneyed man and banker of his day in these parts, having so far outstripped his cotemporaries in shrewdness and enterprise, as to have a special command of the money-market. Starting with only the same means, and with a much more expensive family, he died worth twice as much as the General. Notwithstanding a reputation for the too great love of money, which shrewd men often suffer, he was no niggard of it, either in his domestic or his public concerns, being liberal in his relations to the town and most generous and hospitable in his household. The town votes to accept his offer to frame a bridge, at his own expense, over Cold River, if they will raise and cover it. He did more than any body in the way of personal superintendence, and more in the purchase of pews than any one but the General, towards the erection of the new meeting-house. The votes of the town, respecting that edifice, show that it had, and required his constant attention. There was a great difference of opinion as to where it ought to be placed; and then a great dispute whether it should have a round top or a steeple; and then most vacillating counsels respecting the distribution of the middle of the floor into body seats or pews; but through it all, the Colonel favored liberal counsels and prompt action, and gave time, attention, and money to consummate the large undertaking. It is a pleasant proof of the good taste of the times, that as early as 1792, the town being called on to decide what color it would have the new meeting-house, voted to paint the outside of a *straw-color*. They seem, however, to have had the same ignorance that fences would keep cattle from the precincts of meeting-houses which their descendants suffer from; as the tenth article in the warrant for town-meeting in 1791 is, "To see if the town will come into any method to prevent sheep lying round the new meeting-house;" and at the same meeting the town voted with most ferocious unanimity, "that Asa Gage and Nicanor Townsley take care and keep the dogs out of the meeting-house on Sabbath days, and KILL THEM." An effort continued through many years, and filling no mean space in the town records, to get the burial-ground fenced in, shows that this matter of fencing is a very tardy product of civilization. The burial-ground was neither cleared nor fenced in 1783; for the town votes an inquiry, why Captain Goldsmith, who had engaged to do it, has neglected his duty. In all these matters Colonel John had an active part. He was a very regular attendant at meeting with his whole family, riding invariably on horseback beside the chaise containing his wife and daughters;—a member of the Church and a man of sobriety and dignity.

The Colonel valued himself on his housekeeping. His cellars groaned with the bounties of nature; and from their size and the thoroughness of their masonry seemed fitted to a feudal lord. Eating and drinking were no jokes in those days; and nothing but the hardy out-of-door life our ancestors led will account for their feats at the table. The Colonel would not have known his breakfast if the smoke of a beef-steak were not in his nostrils; nor would the tea-table have been recognized, if a broiled chicken or bacon and eggs had not eked out the usual array of loaves and cakes, pies and pickles. Yet order and deference reigned at his board. He had a natural dignity that commanded respect, and a natural grace that set the example of courtesy. He was specially polite towards his wife, punctiliously inquiring her wants before those of any other person present at table. His daughters waited on him with careful respect; towards the close of his life Harriet pinned on his napkin before dinner, and removed it afterwards without notice. He never entered a house without the then common formula of greeting among courteous and well-bred folks, "Your most obedient," accompanied with a considerable sweep of the hand.

In person, he was five feet nine or ten inches high; of a light or florid complexion; carefully dressed, and a little more haughty and reserved in his bearing than the General. Probably he was a man of more mind but less culture; of less heart and more ambition. His public concerns did not outweigh, as in the General's case, his private interests. With strict rectitude and propriety of life, he was more chargeable with worldliness than his elder brother; but was a valuable, high-minded, and excellent citizen of Walpole. In hospitality he could not be exceeded. The late Dr. Twichell, on a visit to his mansion-house, then occupied by his son Hubbard, said in reference to his recollection of Colonel John's good cheer: "If I should take that house, I should expect to find a roast turkey and a plum-pudding in every cup-board and closet." My own experience, as its present owner, would somewhat disappoint the Doctor's favorable prognostics.

The Colonel had a large family, and one which he very much indulged. His daughters were the most elegant and dressy, and the best-educated young women in these parts; and being of attractive person, drew a gay company to the house. His sons, with the Bellows love of horses, high animal spirits, natural joviality and keen wit, made the town ring with their good-fellowship and dashing ways. The times had not taught prudence, temperance, or the necessity of bringing up the sons of rich men to work; and Colonel John's family was no exception to the universal errors of the day.

Walpole itself was the scene of more roistering and merry-making than would now be credible, at the time the Colonel's children were growing up. A little knot of wits, then living here, attracted the gay and witty society of the whole region round. Keene and Charlestown, Westminster and Brattleboro', sent their contributions. Joe Denny, Jerry Mason, Major Bullard, Roger Vose, Dr. Heiliman, Alpheus Moore, Dr. Spaulding, Royal Tyler, and the like, converted the village tavern into a sort of literary pandemonium, in which fine scholarship, elegant wit, late card-playing, hearty eating, and hard drinking were mingled in a very fascinating complication. The revolutionary army had lately broken up, and thrown many gay and leisurely men upon society. The military men all about knew Major Bullard, and made appointments to meet at his house. The lawyers on their circuits between Keene and Charlestown, made a point of stopping here. There were several of the citizens engaged in trade, whom dealings in furs and with the Indians, had given a habit of travel, and acquaintance with society, that made them highly companionable. Walpole lay on the main road to Canada, and had a relative importance then, it has never possessed since. It is said that a venerable Bishop used to make a point of putting up here, for the sake of a good time with the wits of the place, who were known far and near for their jollity and peculiar culture. Indeed, we have only to remember who they were. Joe Denny wrote here in Walpole in a style of elegance which was unexampled in his day, and which fully entitled him to the name of the American Addison. He was a delicately-made, small man, of a light complexion; needy of purse, but usually dressing in pumps, and white stockings, which it was sometimes said he pulled down day by day into his shoes until there was no more leg to pull. The Portfolio, which he afterwards edited in Philadelphia, contained the remnant of the Lay-Preacher, which he commenced in the Farmer's Museum here; for Walpole had a newspaper as early as 1793, started by Isaiah Thomas in connection with David Carlisle, one of his freed apprentices, and a native of Walpole. A bookstore and publishing office were started here at the same time, from which several very well-printed volumes came forth, which I occasionally meet with, with the Walpole imprint on the title-page. Joseph T. Buckingham was an apprentice in this office. Denny died an early death, caused by intemperance, leaving the memory of splendid talents quenched in the bowl of festivity.

Jerry Mason was not here long. His glorious career at the

bar of New-Hampshire and Massachusetts is well known. Hardly second to Daniel Webster in natural parts, and probably better read in his profession, he adorned the bar and his native State by his sound learning and high character. He stood six feet seven inches in height. It is said that while in this town, travelling across the hills to Keene in a sleigh, a teamster roughly ordered him out of the road, which he had already more than half-abandoned. Mason refused to move further, and the teamster threatened to compel him. Raising his head from the buffalo-robes that concealed him, Mason slowly elevated his person, up, up, up, so far beyond the ordinary height of humanity, that the burly teamster in amazement and fright, exclaimed, "That'll dew—guess I better tarn out myself 'fore there's any more on yer." I have myself conversed some years ago with Mr. Mason concerning his Walpole life, having dined with him, on one occasion, about seventeen years ago, in the village tavern here; and from him I gathered some of the impressions I now seek to communicate.

Royal Tyler, of Brattleboro', became afterwards Chief-Justice of Vermont, and was a man of distinguished abilities and wit. He never lived here, but was a frequent visitor.

Roger Vose was, as you all know, celebrated for the brilliancy of his repartee and the fascination of his good fellowship. He had married the eldest daughter of Colonel John. He is said to have been the original propounder of the comparison, since grown stale from its universal usage, but at first immensely ludicrous, which described the disputed size of a thing, with the highly instructive illustration of its being as big as a piece of chalk. Miss Nancy Pearce had a very small watch, presented by her brother, a successful merchant in Boston, which was a subject of large and curious interest in Walpole; and it was in a high debate touching its size, that the Judge quizzically introduced this original comparison.

He is said, when in Congress, to have replied to a Southern member, who called his attention to a drove of mules passing by their boarding-house, exclaiming, "Look here, Judge; here goes a company of your constituents!" "Yes, yes," said the Judge; "I see—going South, to be ministers and schoolmasters."

"Who are you in mourning for?" said the Judge to one of his gay students, who entered the office one morning in what was then not so common as now, a suit of black. "My sins only," answered the young blade. "I did'nt know you'd lost any," sympathizingly responded the Judge.

When the famous cannon case was decided against Walpole at the Keene Court, the victors immediately dragged out the gun and fired it off. "The case is already reported, may it please your honor," said Counsellor Vose.

But I can not dwell upon these recollections. Suffice it to say, that Walpole has improved immensely in sobriety since those times. Then, suppers of bear's meat and venison, of oysters and other imported delicacies, were very common at the public tavern; at which punch and other inebriating drinks were as freely used as water. It was not an uncommon thing for these festivities to end in very riotous scenes; the tables and chairs being occasionally broken in pieces and built into a bon-fire in the middle of the floor. What became of dishes and pitchers, I leave you to surmise. Indeed, it is within my recollection, that the village-tavern was the centre of all amusement; the bowling-alley there being the afternoon and evening resort, and punch for the company the regular indulgence. I have heard a shrewd observer say, that forty years ago, the rum alone sold in Walpole caused more trade than now exists in the town.

Card-playing was then carried to an absurd excess, and often extended into the early hours of the next morning. Even the dignity of Parson Fessenden did not save him from a nick-name among these wicked wits, drawn from their favorite game of Lu. In reference to his short figure, cocked hat, and peculiar gait, they profanely styled him after the jack of clubs —the most important card, as I learn, in the game of Lu— "Old Pam"—

> "Even mighty *Pam* that kings and queens o'erthrew,
> And mowed down armies in the fights of *Lu*."

Rape of the Lock, lines 61 *and* 62.

I must not omit to say, that Parson Fessenden was a rare man both in character and talents, of eminent purity, excellent professional learning, and marked originality of mind. His "Science of Sanctity" was, for the times, a book of high ability, and fresh, unborrowed thought. He contends in it, with singular courage and fidelity, for many opinions then very heretical, but since extensively held by the best minds. His intellect was keen, careful, and solid; his heart just, pure, and true. He possessed a moral liberality far in advance of his day, and his writings breathe a love of liberty, a preference of realities over all pretenses, which show him to have been a person of fine nature and noble character. His memory ought to be precious and venerable in the town he fed so long with the bread of life.

Colonel John died in 1812. Shortly before his death he told his nephew, Mr. Abel Bellows, that he was prepared to go, and would not turn over his hand to stay. Just previous to his decease he was heard to exclaim, "The world is no more for me."*

Colonel Joseph Bellows, my own grand-father, was the next son of the old Colonel. He was born June 6, 1744, married Lois Whitney, had fourteen children, and died May 13, 1817. His early promise was at least as good as that of either of his brothers, and was sufficiently evinced in the confidence of his father, who sent him, at eighteen years of age, to Lunenberg, to take care of the valuable farm he had left. He soon

* Walpole had in	1749	1	family.	
" "	1759	4	families.	
" "	1767	308	inhabitants.	
" "	1775	658	"	
" "	1790	1245	"	
" "	1800	1743	"	
" "	1810	1894	"	
" "	1820	2020	"	and no change since.

The most rapid growth was from 1767 to 1800, when the Colonel's children were all actively on the stage. It has grown little or none since.

In 1805, there were 4800 barrels of cider made in town, and about 1800 inhabitants, and all drunk in the place, being about three barrels to each man, woman, and child! Colonel John had the largest orchard in town, 30 acres of apple-trees.

In 1820, the production of cider had fallen off to 1225 barrels. 40,000 lbs. of butter, 60,000 lbs. cheese, 110,000 lbs. of beef, 180,000 lbs. pork, 5500 lbs. flax.

The bridge was built at the Falls by Colonel Enoch Hale, in 1785.

NEWSPAPERS IN WALPOLE.

Farmers' Museum.
The Political Observatory, published by George W. Nichols, 1803–1808.
Cheshire Gazette, started at Walpole, 1825, lived one year.
Farmers' Museum, renewed 1827, removed to Keene.

NEWSPAPERS IN KEENE.

Keene had a newspaper, New-Hampshire Recorder, in 1787–1791.
Cheshire Advertiser, 1792, one year.
Columbian Informer, 1793–1795.
The Rising Sun, 1795–1798.
New-Hampshire Sentinel, 1799.

became a man of influence in the part of Massachusetts in which he resided; took, it is said, the chief direction of town affairs, and was generally selected as referee in matters of dispute among his neighbors. In the revolution, he was appointed to superintend the drafting of men from that district. I possess the original commission from Gov. Hancock, appointing him Lieutenant-Colonel; and he went with Colonel Ben's regiment to Ticonderoga, captured some Indians, and brought home various trophies in the shape of wampum, brooches, etc. I think he was out in the Shay's rebellion. He used to amuse his grand-children by recounting the scenes of his early military life, in a way to impress their imaginations very much. In the course of his various and extensive dealings, Colonel Joe became bondsman for Messrs. Hutchins & Fowler, (contractors with the government, I suppose,) and through them became embarrassed. In 1784, his property was attached. His health had been poor during that year, and his losses acting upon his excessive pride of character, and solicitude for his family, which was uncommonly strong, broke down the powers of his mind, and reduced him to insanity.

The moment this dreadful news reached Walpole, his brothers, the General and the Colonel, both hastened to Lunenberg,* to make the best arrangement of his affairs, and to look after their unfortunate brother and his family. Colonel Joe's insanity, although not always visible to strangers, continued to the very close of his life; mild in its ordinary character, but sometimes violent. He possessed a delicate, affectionate, and elevated disposition; was humane and religious; delighted in the prattle of children, and in the recital of hymns. He could not bear cruelty in any form, and was especially sensitive to the sufferings, real or imaginary, of children. The great and ever-memorable kindness of his brothers should be carefully treasured in the hearts of my

* My father's next brother, Uncle Ben, still living in a hale old age, remembers that he, a boy of a dozen years, brought the intelligence of his father's insanity to Walpole, on horse-back; that although it was Sunday, the General, scrupulous as he was, started off that afternoon in a double-sleigh for Lunenberg, having despatched a messenger to Exeter, to inform Colonel John of the calamity. He immediately left his public duties there, came back to Walpole, and started off in another double sleigh for my poor grand-father's house. In these two conveyances the children of the family were brought to Walpole.

grandfather's descendants, and I have felt in some degree like returning an old debt, in thus seeking to brighten the memories of those who succored the helplessness of my own immediate ancestor. These excellent brothers brought the whole family to Walpole—very large as it was—and distributed it about among the uncles, aunts, and cousins, as room could be made. I have heard one of my uncles say, within a few months, that he should never forget the tones with which Colonel John's oldest daughter, Rebecca, said, as he was brought in and laid with his cold feet to the fire, being a mere child, and she supposing him to be asleep, "Poor homeless boy, how I pity him!" Colonel Joe was blessed with a wife, and his children with a mother, of rare equanimity and sweetness of temper. Like other insane men, his mind running always on the sufferings and prospective or imaginary wants of his children, conceived a prejudice against his best friend, the wife he had most tenderly loved; and this went to such an extent, that they rarely lived together after his disease became fixed. The children, early thrown upon their own resources, soon showed signs of enterprise and independence. Their father's ruin was the making of them. He lived to see them fully able to provide for each other, and for him; and their mother in a benign old age, beloved and honored, surrounded by children, grandchildren, and great-grand-children, passed away the object of devoted love and unbounded respect. The recollection of her smile is among my most treasured memories. I saw it in my father's face, when, a week after his death, I went from New-York to Boston, and opened the family tomb to look once again upon his remains. The weather was cold, and he remained unchanged; and his mother's peaceful smile fixed upon his marble lips, spoke of the rest he had gone to enjoy with her in heaven. Colonel Joe was 73 years and 11 months old when he died. I have sometimes thought that his delicate nervous temperament had been extensively inherited by his descendants, and that they might owe their love of music, their tendency to reflection, and their relative love of books, to a constitution somewhat more nervous than muscular. However that may be, I believe that out of perhaps twenty descendants of the old Founder who have since had the advantage of a liberal education, two thirds of the whole number have been descendants of Colonel Joseph. Happily, his insanity was not of an hereditary character; afflicting, so far as I know, no one of his children or grand-children.

We come now to the children of Colonel Bellows's second wife, Mary Hubband. She died Feb. 21, 1794; and the Walpole newspaper of that date speaks of her thus:

"Died, in this town, the 21st inst., Madam Mary Bellows, in the 69th year of her age, relict of the late Colonel Benjamin Bellows. As he had been a father, and chief-proprietor of the town, so she was a mother in our Israel. She was a woman of exemplary piety, who made it her endeavor to keep a conscience void of offense both towards God and man; a steady attendant upon the public worship of God, and observer of the institutions of the Gospel; an excellent economist, and a charitable friend to the industrious poor. In her the town hath lost one who contributed much in her sphere to the building of it up in its infant state. As a wife she loved and reverenced her husbands, and in her widowhood behaved with wisdom and propriety. She was an indulgent as well as exemplary parent to her numerous descendants, who have cause to rise up and call her blessed. 'Blessed are the dead that die in the Lord, and their memory is precious.' Her funeral was attended on the 25th, by a great concourse of people, from within town and without.

"In faith she died, in dust she lies;
But faith foresees that dust shall rise
When Jesus calls, while Hope assumes,
And boast her joy among the tombs."

Abigail was born Jan. 13, 1759, and married for her first husband Colonel Seth Hunt, of Northampton, by whom she had one son, the well-known Colonel Seth Hunt, of this town, a man of singularly fine manners, and who with some slight changes of fortune or character, would have achieved a very distinguished place in society. Her second husband was Captain Richardson, of Keene, by whom she had also one child, killed by being thrown with its mother from a horse, on the road between Keene and Walpole.

Aunt Richardson has lived within our own day, and we all know that she did not outlive her wit, her activity, her independence of feeling. She was a gay and buoyant girl, full of pranks and high spirits, and many are the recollections of her practical jokes and witticisms. When a girl, she possessed a beautiful saddle-horse, her father's gift, of which she was not a little proud. She had trained her horse in such a way that when patted on a certain place in the neck, he grew suddenly restive, and commenced rearing and prancing in a way to exhibit her horsemanship to great advantage and with little danger. When yet a young lady, she rode this horse down to Lunenberg, on a visit to her brother Joseph. While at his house, he buried an infant son, and on occasion of the funeral there proved to be some lack of horses to carry all the party to the burial-ground, and a certain serving-maid, one Sarah Anne, at her brother's request, was placed behind Miss Abigail on a pillion. She was not a little chagrined at finding her favorite converted into a family nag, and her horsemanship put at such disadvantage, and although unable to refuse at the moment the load assigned her, she said, (afterwards,) "I knew I should never carry Sarah Anne, if the boy laid above ground all summer." She rode, however, to the horse-block, and the maid mounted behind her. The procession moved on, when suddenly Miss Abigail's horse was seized with an unaccountable restiveness; and reared and plunged until Sarah Anne was thrown off. Miss Abigail returned very soberly to the horse-block, and Sarah Anne, with her rumpled feathers, was placed in her seat again. A second time the procession started; a second time the vicious beast threw up his heels, and a second time Sarah Anne came to the ground. The third experiment had the same result, until poor Sarah Anne concluded to give up the melancholy ride, and Miss Abigail achieved her somewhat misplaced and mischievous victory.

Her wit continued fresh through life. She had a merry twinkle in her eye, even after it was dimmed with age. Her energy was equal to her spirits. She kept house to the last day of her long life, and only resigned the keys when her breath was but a few hours in her body.

Her last husband, a worthy man, with a little of the Betty in him, sometimes encountered her gentle remonstrances for meddling with her domestic concerns; and on one occasion she threatened him, that when he died, she would bury him in the ash-hole with his head out, that he might continue to know what was going on in the kitchen. She used to say at the last, referring to her want of heirs, and as an apology for giving away her substance freely, that "She did not care to leave so much as a door-latch." Her serious qualities were, I believe, admirable; for humor is an excellent ingredient, and a capital indication, of character. It kept her green to the last. She was charitable and pious, and had a great attachment to the family recollections, and to the old home. She came to Walpole, as she said, that she might die among her kindred, and here she spent several peaceful years with the friends of her youth, and here she died and was buried, leaving no descendants, her son dying before her, unmarried.

Theodore, eldest son of the second set of children, was born Aug. 13, 1760, in the fort; he and his sister Abigail being the only children of the family born there.

When first married, he lived in this town, in a house the site of which is on what is now Mr. Knapp's farm; it was standing within my recollection; and the lot was, and is still, called in memory of him, "the Uncle Thod. lot." At the age of twenty, I find by one of the army rolls* that he was a sergeant in Capt. P. Page's company of militia, raised by New Hampshire in 1780, (Col. Nichols's regiment,) to join the continental army for the defense of West Point; and that he served three months and fourteen days. He was 17 years old when his father died, and probably never had much control exercised over him. Being of a huge frame and lively spirits, he was convivial in his habits, and not above the prevailing indulgences of the day in which he lived. Misfortunes overtook his property, but he had the blessing of a good and constant brother in "the Squire," who never failed to minister to his necessities. He was a man of an easy nature, and as he himself would have given freely, he did not scruple to receive as freely. He lived the latter part of his life in Charlestown, N. H. He, more than any one of our Founder's children, emulated his father in size and weight; attaining, I believe, over 300 lbs. He possessed immense bodily strength in his prime; and a nearly incredible story, for which, however, living witnesses vouch, relates that on a certain occasion, when a trial was made of the strength of some horses, by hitching them in turn to the great iron cannon, and no one of them could drag it from its position, Uncle Thod slipped his head into the collar, and alone drew the weight which no horse had been able to stir! Whether or no he had any thing to do with the famous strife about the cannon, which arose between

* Vol. 3, Letter K, page 16.

Walpole and Keene, I can not tell, but he was just the man to have entered heart and soul into that controversy, even though near fifty years old at the time. It seems that each of the four forts on Connecticut River had been supplied with a large iron cannon, by his Majesty the King of England. These cannon remaining after our independence in the several towns where the forts had been, were prized as trophies, and used for purposes of rejoicing on public days. The neighboring towns became jealous of the gun-towns, and, in 1807, some citizens of Keene, led by a young officer, afterwards distinguished in the service of his country, determined to repair to Walpole in the night, and steal the cannon from its unguarded gun-house. This they accomplished. The Walpolians indignantly protested, and attempted to arrest the ringleader in the offense, but in vain. They sought the aid of the law, but the Court decided that the said cannon was not the property of the town, and the defendants were discharged.

Very much irritated, the Walpolians resolved on a recapture of their trophy. They had discovered that it was concealed in a granary in a back store on the south side of West street. On the evening of the 4th July, 1809, a plot was laid to accomplish their purpose. A confederate, a stage-driver, was sent to Keene in a huge stage-wagon, under the pretense of buying grain, but in reality to discover and arrange for the recapture. He learned the place of its concealment, bargained for his grain, and obtained possession of the key of the place where it was stored, under the plea of taking in his grain very early the next morning, without disturbing the clerks. This done, he went a little way out of town, and met in the dark a cavalcade of thirty Walpole men, led by an officer of high militia rank, and made his report. Tieing their horses in the bushes, they stole into town, made their way to the granary, and after desperate efforts, succeeded in lifting the gun into their wagon, and started off at a spanking pace for Walpole. The noise of the rescue had, however, aroused some of the people, who rang the town-bell and raised the alarm. A large party of Keene men mounted their horses and started in hot pursuit; but luckily they took the wrong road, and thus, perhaps, a perilous conflict was avoided. At break of day, the Walpole band were welcomed by the ringing of the village bell, and by the applause of a crowd of their anxious townsmen, who had all night been awaiting their return. This same cannon was afterwards stolen by a party from Westminster, Vt., for use on the Fourth of July, and retaken by our citizens while in actual service. It was again taken by men from Alstead; and report says, after that, appropriated by an iron founder, and transmuted into implements of husbandry.

Uncle Theodore, after a long life, died from the effects of a violent blow received from the swinging to of a barn-door. His descendants are numerous, and highly respectable. A prosperous branch of his family settled at Newburgh, on the Hudson River; and some of the race indulge the original passion for horses, by keeping excellent livery stables in the city of New York.

Thomas, the second son of those born in Walpole, was born Sept. 17, 1762, the year the family homestead was erected, which he finally inherited from his father. Why the old Colonel left this estate to Thomas, (only 15 years old at his death,) and not to Theodore, Josiah, or some other of his sons, I do not know; but it looks as if he foresaw the prudence, good sense, and general fitness of his son Thomas to hold that valuable, and to the founder of it, undoubtedly, highly prized estate. His son valued the gift at more than its pecuniary worth, and held it through his life undivided, as he thought his father would have wished him to do. It continues, I suppose to the pecuniary disadvantage, but also to the high moral enjoyment of its owner, his son, to be carefully protected from any partitions, not absolutely unavoidable, and saved from the market as the old cradle of the race. We may all rejoice that the venerable house is still guarded from decay, and has only recently renewed its youth, while the beautiful meadows and broad pastures about it wear the same family aspect we have known them by so long. I never pass by without a mental raising of my hat.

The first notice I find of Uncle Thomas, in the town records, is under date March 15, 1780, when a worthy citizen enters his formal protest against Theodore and Thomas Bellows voting, being yet minors. To catch the Squire doing any thing illegal, even at the gay age of eighteen, surprises those who knew that his honesty was native, not cultivated, and that he did not know how to do wrong. When Mr. Knapp once bantered him upon this discovery of his early misdemeanor, he justified himself fully, saying that he voted not in right of his age, but in right of his property, which we believe was, under the laws of that time, a good defense.

I find him styled in the town records, Lieutenant Thomas, in '91; and it is an evidence of his early weight of character, that, notwithstanding his well-remembered infirmity of speech, he was appointed Moderator in his 29th year. The next year he was sent representative. In '94, appointed counsellor to the Governor, for five years; and in '99, sheriff of the county, an office which he held for more than thirty years, without an imputation on his fidelity, and with as little hard feeling as was ever excited by any occupant of that post. Meanwhile he filled every sort of town office, and was a most efficient citizen. As General Bellows seemed to take the old Colonel's place, so at his death, the Sheriff took his in the confidence and respect of the town. A most simple-hearted, honest, pure, and benevolent man was Thomas Bellows. Careful of the poor, kind and constant to his friends, no lover of money, not covetous of rapid or unjust gains, quick to perceive the right, and anxious only to do it, he passed a blameless and respected life.

Who does not know the Squire? His wonderful memory of names and dates, with the endless store of anecdotes of the past—a memory which carried down with it into the grave an unspeakable treasury of facts now lost for ever; his childlike curiosity—the fruit of lively interest in his townsmen—which made him ask so many home-questions; his pride of character, so free from all worldly ambition or parade; his punctilious discharge of every trust and duty; his paternal concern for all the members of the Bellows race, and the inquisitive interest with which he followed their respective careers through the world. I can see his tall and broad figure, with his white neckcloth and pepper-and-salt clothes, leaning over the pew at meeting, in time of prayer, with no affectation of closed eyes, or special sanctity of visage, but with perfect respect to the occasion. He did not know how to put any thing on. Again, I see him in his wagon, jogging through the town, and stopping with kindly sympathy to chat a moment with each person he met, and tell his own business and find out theirs.

How many trusts he held, how many orphans looked up to him as a father, how many widows leaned upon his honest arm, you all know. Without special powers of intellect, he had so honest and true a heart, that all respected his judgment and loved his counsel. The natural impediment in his speech seemed almost appropriate to the unworldly simplicity of his character. At any rate it completed the triumph of his worth; for it never diminished the respect in which he was held, or, however playfully mimicked, had any power to lessen the just and universal regard of his fellow-citizens. The Squire was too guileless, open, and childlike to possess any other dignity than that of purity and goodness. It seems almost a contradiction of his mild, peace-making, and affectionate nature, to think of him as high-sheriff; but he had all the force of character necessary to any duty he assumed.

I could furnish numerous anecdotes illustrative of the Squire's character. But he has too recently gone from us, and has left too many children here, to make it becoming to say more. Besides, who, not of our youngest children, does not remember the Squire? And who that ever saw did not see through him, and behold within and without a spotless, whole-hearted, kind and worthy man, not unfitted to illustrate and perpetuate his father's name and character?

Aunt Kinsley, Mary Bellows, the youngest daughter of the old Colonel, was a woman of uncommon native force of intellect and power of character. She was cast in that mould of the female nature which would have fitted her to be the wife of some resolute old Puritan, in the days when wives buckled on their husband's swords and bade them die, but not dishonor their name and faith. Tall and commanding in person, firm and original in her opinions, of native dignity and elevation, free from frivolous tastes or feminine weaknesses, she carried self-respect with her all her days, and secured the veneration even more than the love of others. Those, however, more intimately acquainted with her domestic life, speak gratefully of the depth of tenderness held in her heart, and of the power she possessed to win the warm affections of others. She was efficient in benevolence from principle and inclination. Possessing unusual business capacity and large experience, she managed her affairs with discretion, and was a help-meet indeed to her husband, whose Congressional life carried him much away from home. She was not the ordinary type of the Bellows race, which leans more to mercy than justice, and is rather distinguished for the tender and humane than for the heroic and celestial graces. A certain spontaneous sympathy, ready to burst out at the sight of suffering or wrong, is natural to the race. Its goodness is usually more a matter of instinct than of cultivation; of feeling than principle; but Aunt Kinsley seemed to be rather an exception to the rule, and to possess a mind accustomed to weigh its conclusions, govern its emotions, and regulate itself by a deliberate principle. She belonged to the severer school of religion, and did honor to her faith in her practice. Our family would have done more and better if a larger infusion of the element represented in Mary's life had been poured into it. Force of feeling has governed it more than force of will. Both are essential to the truest development of humanity.

Mrs. Kinsley, after the death of her husband, resided chiefly in the family of her only child, Mrs. Gardiner; but after her grand-children, early bereft of a most interesting mother, ceased to need her care, she followed the family instinct of her race, and repaired to Walpole to end her days. Here, in the society of her brother, the Squire, and with the charge of his household, she passed several years of tranquil usefulness, forming a most important element in her brother's happiness in his old age; and here, in the enjoyment of a firm religious faith, and with a venerated memory, she closed her eyes.

I recollect, as a boy, the visits of Judge Kinsley and his wife to my father's house in Boston; his gentlemanly and courteous appearance and manners; her stories of life in Maine, where they then lived, which made a wild and romantic impression on me. How much I have regretted, in preparing these offhand sketches, the neglect of the now-lost opportunity of collecting from the mouths of these original witnesses their recollections of the early life of our town and family! But unhappily, I did not know how to ask questions until it was too late. One hour with the Squire, or with Aunt Kinsley, or Aunt Richardson would have been invaluable to me in the preparation of these family notes.

Josiah, the youngest child of the old Colonel, was ten years old when his father died, and grew up with the children of his elder brothers. He enjoyed better opportunities of education than his brothers, I suppose from being born into a more settled society, and might have had even better ones than he used if he had been disposed to improve them. Old General Bradlee used to tell of his recollections of once seeing Uncle Si and Colonel John's oldest son, while yet boys of sixteen, travel-worn and weary, laboring with their packs, past his house in Westminster, on their way up to the ferry that crossed to the old homestead. Hailing the boys, he found that they had made their way on foot all the way back from New-Haven, whither they had been formally sent on horseback to college. Impatient of the confinement and dull routine of the place, yearning for the large freedom and exciting life of their half-redeemed forest-home, they had run away from college, and were ready to face any amount of domestic reproach rather than endure its unnatural bondage. It was probably quite as well for the boys; for unwilling pupils learn very little except dissipation within college walls, and these boys had spirits that were not likely to escape explosion.

I have heard, what my own recollections of the dignity and sobriety of my father's youngest uncle, his cotemporary in years, makes it almost impossible for me to credit, that Uncle Josiah had a prankish and gay humor in his youth, and was hail-fellow well-met with the blades and ne'er-do-wells of the time; that matrimony, which cures so many of our faults, corrected all his, and made him the sober, wise, and careful citizen he was. Certain it is his life, within the recollection of most of us, was worthy of all imitation for its industry, gravity, public-spirit, and domestic fidelity. There was a singular simplicity and force about Uncle Si; no man ever suspected him of any cant, pretense, or sentimentality, and no one, I suspect, ever approached him with any under-hand or cunning scheme. Though somewhat reserved, he was plain to bluntness in the expression of his opinion when it was sought or needed, and his opinion was always valuable for its round-about good sense and foundation in experience. An excellent farmer, his example and advice influenced the agriculture of the place; a good citizen, he always lent a generous support to every public interest, the church, the school, and the administration of the town. He was a man of marked modesty, never obtruding himself, and resigning rather than craving public place. His home was populous with children and children's children, and had no fault except that being blessed chiefly with daughters it did not leave more sons like their father. In modern days, Walpole has had few men on whom it leaned so much as on Uncle Josiah. The people at large respected so much his integrity and his judgment, his plain good sense, and his unpretending honesty, that he wielded a wide and enviable influence. His children, better educated than their father, always experienced the natural force of his character, and had the happiness to feel that deference and respect, which, though it be purchased with some show of sternness, is so much better than the offensive familiarity now often seen between the young and the old of the same household. Uncle Si, I always knew, had a tender heart, and was only too much ashamed of his better feelings and softer emotions—a fault which belonged to my own father—or rather, not so much a fault as a peculiarity of the Puritan ancestry from which they sprung, and the somewhat heroic lives they early lived. The youngest son of the old Colonel's family did not dishonor his origin, and his children and grand-children may well cherish the memory of their father, so much and so respectfully recollected in his native town. "Uncle Si," that phrase so familiar to my youth, was always the synonym of honesty, firmness, judgment, and promptness—of self-respect, independence, and modest worth. Peace to his ashes, and prosperity to his worthy race!

And thus, kinsmen and friends, I have brought to a conclusion, what I designed, a sketch of the lives and characters of our Founder and his children.

I shall be much disappointed if you are not ready to unite with me in expressions of gratitude and satisfaction, that God has given us so pure, so strong, and so wholesome an origin. Our ancestors have occupied just that station in life from which the best and most healthy blood, the strongest and most lasting respectability, flows. They have been plain, substantial farmers, dignified with sufficient education and breeding to escape coarseness, conversant enough with public station and the world to be emancipated from local prejudices and narrowness; but neither educated enough, rich enough, nor widely-known enough to encounter the perils of political elevation, domestic luxury, or conventional refinement.

Robust in body and practical in understanding, humane in heart and simple in manners, they have founded a race of which they need not be ashamed, and given us ancestors of which we may justly be proud.

They have belonged to the working-class in the truest sense, and have been genuine republicans and hearty Americans, mixing always freely and evenly with their fellow-beings. An honest pride of character has ever distinguished them. I never heard of one of the name who was convicted of a criminal offense. Their faults have been those springing from good-fellowship and a constitutional strength of appetite. We have, alas! furnished our full contribution to the ranks of intemperance, when it was the vice of the country and the age; but setting that great weakness aside, I know of none other from which our skirts are not as clean as those of any family of equal size in the country. I never heard a hoarding, mean, and selfish spirit charged upon our race. It has been distinguished for hospitality, for public spirit, and for general success in life; and I thank God, with you, that there is at present no appearance of decline either in its numbers, its character, or its reputation.

We should have come together to very little purpose at this time, were our only object that of self-glorification, or even friendly intercourse. Those who still live on the native hills where our race was cradled and nursed, have called the clan together from all parts of its dispersion, to animate the common virtue and resolution of each and all by grateful meditations on its past history; that by considering our origin and parentage, we may be moved to self-respect, and to new and more resolute endeavors to shed lustre on the family name.

That generation that binds those of us now upon the active stage of life, and our children, to the founders and fathers of our race, is now fast leaving the scene; and it is a most pleasant reflection, that they have lived to see their children rise up and call their parents blessed. More than seventy years have elapsed since our Founder died; and of course those whose infant eyes saw the last of him, are now just closed, or fast closing in death. Still a few veterans linger in the neighborhood of four-score, the eye and ear-witnesses of the men and the events I have described, cotemporaries not of our Founder, but of his children. This is to them a proud and happy day; and their presence is the chief charm of this occasion to us, their juniors and children. Let us assure them, before they leave the world, that we will not dishonor their name and race; that we receive as a precious inheritance the traditions and reputation of the family; that Walpole, the creation of our Founder and his children, shall be our Mecca and Jerusalem; that we will look to it as the natural home of our declining years, and the sweetest resting-place for our ashes. Let us shrive their spirits, now ready to depart, with the sacred promise, that we will dwell in peace and unity as a family, mutually helpful in times of misfortune, solicitous to defend each other's reputation and virtue, and anxiously devoted to whatever can honor and exalt the name of our race. Such promises will add to the peace of their dying beds.

Cousins! hail and farewell. A few days will find you again at your scattered posts of duty. Meanwhile, we welcome you to the homestead and the old hearth-stone. Look upon our hills. Are there fairer ones on the face of the earth? Our meadows. Spread there anywhere more peaceful and fertile intervals? Our river. Flows there a more silvery tide, changeful yet constant, winding but onward, wild and yet gentle? This home our Progenitor chose and rescued from the wilderness for his children and theirs. Look upon our elm-shaded streets, our places of worship, our school-houses, and our homes. The foundation of all this beauty, prosperity, and civilization our honored Father laid with his brave, strong hand. Do we not owe his memory all the honors we can pay it, and his children, our more immediate parents, the praise of well sustaining what he so well begun?

Go to the scene of the old fort, and the ancient homestead; to the terraces, now so peaceful, on which the Kilburn fight took place; to the places where the General and Colonel John have left their strong mark and pleasant impressions; above all, go to the Great Fall. In all you will find occasions of joy and gratitude for what the fathers have done. Yonder marble monument is a fitting tribute to the worth which created from the forest so fair and rich a scene as this—which originated a race such as has gathered around it. But a righteous Providence was before-hand with us, and had anticipated the fitting memorial of our honored ancestor. The Falls themselves—Bellows Falls—they are the everlasting memorial of him who chose their neighborhood for his home, and the home of his race. Everlasting—because while their waters continue to be replenished from the snows of distant mountains and the contributions of a thousand streams, their name is embodied in the topography and history of our country and the world. They bear his name as far as the sound of the English language is known, and will hand it down as long as it lasts. Bursting through mountain-walls, and falling on rocks, they fitly typify his resolute spirit, which no obstacles could hinder, no hardships break. Beautiful waters, we have seen, is the etymological purport of our family fame. The Falls do but repeat their own praise in taking the name of their founder.

The old crest, an arm raised to pour water from a chalice into a basin, anticipated the ornament of our Walpole Home, and the natural feature with which our family name is alone publicly associated—Bellows Falls. Let us make that crest universal and honorable, symbolical and Christian. "Whoso giveth a cup of cold water, only in the name of a disciple, shall in no wise lose his reward." Type of purity, of truth, of abundance, we adopt the cup of water, taken from our Founder's Falls, as the family crest, and with it, that beautiful motto, so pious and so expressive:

"All from on high."
(Tout d'en Haut)

"Every good and perfect gift cometh down from above." God gave us our fathers, and while the waters pour over the Great Fall of our river, we will not forget them, or Him.

APPENDIX.

AN ACCOUNT OF THE FAMILY MEETING.

The descendants of Col. Benjamin Bellows, the founder of Walpole, wishing to erect in the New Cemetery a monument to the virtues of their ancestor, issued, by their committee, a circular address to all the known members of the family, stating the object, and requesting their coöperation. The invitation was accepted with cheerful promptitude. The sum of $1200 was raised, and afterward an additional sum of $300. Early in October, the monument, made of Italian marble, twenty feet in height, with appropriate inscriptions, and with figures emblematic of the frontier life, beautifully sculptured, was erected by Bowker, Torrey & Co., of Boston.

On the 11th of October, the descendants came from the north, south, east, and far west, to join in consecrating, with filial veneration, this moumental memorial to their ancestor. They met in the cemetery, at the foot of the monument. The weather was delightful. The design of the meeting was announced by Benjamin Bellows Grant, Esq., the judicious, energetic, and indefatigable chairman of the committee, super intendent of the work and of subsequent arrangements.

The exercises were commenced with a devout and strikingly appropriate prayer, by the Rev. John N. Bellows, of Wilton. A short address was then made by the Rev. Dr. Henry W. Bellows, of New-York; an original hymn followed; and the exercises at the cemetery were closed with an earnest prayer and benediction by the Rev. Mr. Tilden, of Walpole. The meeting then moved to the town-hall, where many had already assembled. Expectation sat with ready ears and excited anticipations for the speaker, Dr. Bellows, to begin his address. He held the audience in riveted attention for three hours. The address was replete with local history, biographical sketches, amusing anecdotes, humorous allusions, and just remarks. It was delivered with those various modulations of voice, occasional playful expressions of countenance, ease and elegance for which he is distinguished.

The relatives and invited guests than passed into the lower hall, a spacious room, which was tastefully decorated with evergreens. A collation had been prepared by a committee of ladies, with skill and elegance, and with a profusion worthy of the olden days of Walpole, when its hills and meadows flowed with milk and honey. After fasting from breakfast until four o'clock, a blessing being asked, the company, with no doubtful appetites, performed their parts in a manner worthy the example of their healthy ancestors.

When the repast was finished, sentiments, speeches, and odes followed, and were continued into the evening.

From the collation, many of the company, by an invitation given to all, spent the remaining part of the evening at the house of Dr. Bellows. His spacious rooms were filled. Friends met there who had not seen one another for years. Mutual congratulations, pleasant recognitions, agreeable introductions to new connections, affectionate inquiries, and interesting reminiscences were crowded into a few hours. Some returned to their homes on the following morning. Those who remained, spent the day in social calls, and in visiting the spots endeared to them by recollections of their childhood, or in hunting up the old fort and the battle-grounds of Indian warfare. Some went to view Bellows Falls; others, the old burying-ground, to find the graves of relatives and friends, and to read the tomb-stone annals of the early settlers—

"Men to fortune and to fame unknown.

"Oft did the harvest to their sickle yield;
Their furrows oft the stubborn glebe has broke.
How jocund did they drive their team a-field!
How bowed the woods beneath their sturdy stroke!"

On Friday morning, nearly all those remaining from abroad, left for home, much gratified with the warm welcome which they had received, and that they had visited the spot consecrated by so many tender recollections.

The following is a copy of the circular:

"*Circular addressed to the Descendants of Col. Benjamin Bellows.*

"WALPOLE, N. H., 1853.

To ——:

"DEAR COUSIN: Many of the descendants of Col. Benjamin Bellows, deeply impressed with their obligations to the father of their family, and the founder of the beautiful town, Walpole, have for many years contemplated the pleasure and duty of erecting, in connection with their relatives absent from the homestead, a monument to his worthy name, near the spot where his ashes repose. The recent consecration of the cemetery (an enlargement of the grave-yard) has revived the interest of the whole town in the memories of its dead, and brought the indefinite project of a monument to its founder to a direct point in the intentions of his descendants.

"At a recent meeting, held at the village-inn, where several branches of the family were represented, after a full comparison of views, a committee was appointed to procure an appropriate design, with an estimate of the expense, and to report upon the best method of obtaining the coöperation of all Col. Bellows's descendants, in the proposed tribute to his memory. The present circular embodies the results, and completes the suggestions of this committee.

"A table of all the living descendants has been made; and, in reviewing their number and character, we have experienced an honest pride which every member of the race is entitled to share and to express; an honest pride which the united family, we trust, will eagerly join to make public, permanent, and inspiring, by a monumental tribute to its father and head, Col. Benjamin Bellows, who, a little more than a hundred years ago, obtained a grant of a township of land, and founded Walpole; and, for many years, struggled with eminent prudence and success with the hardships of a frontier settlement, aggravated by the fierce border-conflicts of the French and Indian wars, during which he frequently displayed the personal heroism of the distinguished partisan, and the prudent skill of a veteran commander; detecting by his sagacity the stratagems of the wily savages, and by his commanding presence and cool courage, exciting their fears and defeating their attacks.

"An extensive block-house on a rich meadow of the Connecticut, was his fortress and dwelling, and gave to the passing stranger protection, a bountiful board, and a hearty welcome, prompted by a hospitality inborn and generous, but unostentatious.

"His great and enduring energy and sound judgment enabled him to overcome every obstacle; and, by his efforts and fostering care, the infant settlement grew and flourished; and, by his example of industry, integrity, and love of good government, he implanted in it the vital principles of continued growth. He has bequeathed to his posterity an unsullied name, and a bright example of integrity, truth, and duty.

"In this contemplated monument we aim at two objects—gratitude to our ancestor, and justice to future descendants. The character of the man forbids alike meanness and ostentation in his memorial; and we have sought to avoid both these extremes in our plan. We have no desire to present him as a national benefactor, nor our family as one of notoriety; but self-respect and an affectionate veneration for our ancestor justify and require a dignified memorial.

"The design exhibits an obelisk of Italian marble, twenty feet in height, with inscriptions and emblems on the four sides, symbolical of Col. Bellows's history as a pioneer and founder. The estimated cost, including an iron fence, is twelve hundred dollars.

"It is manifestly desirable to extend the opportunity of contributing to this monument—as a privilege too sacred to be withheld—to each and every descendant of our founder. This circular is therefore sent to every known descendant of Col. Bellows. We ask a hearty, immediate response from every man, woman, and child, in the form of a contribution to the monument-fund, larger or smaller, as ability or feeling shall warrant or demand. We shall be sadly mistaken in the public-spirit, generous enterprise, and family feeling, if any apathy or difficulty is met with in securing the means for so honorable a purpose.

"Any surplus in the fund may be appropriated by those present at the consecration of the monument, at which time it is proposed to have a general family gathering at the home of our ancestors.

"In bonds of blood and hereditary affection,

"We subscribe ourselves,

"Your friends and kinsmen,

"Benjamin Bellows Grant,
"A. Herbert Bellows,
"Frederick Vose,
"David Buffum,
"Isaac F. Bellows,
"Philip Peck,
"F. N. Knapp."

ORDER OF EXERCISES.

[*At the Cemetery.*]

1. Words of Welcome, by the Chairman of the Committee of Arrangements, B. B. Grant, Esq.

2. Consecrating Address, by Dr. Bellows.

3. Prayer of Consecration, by Rev. John N. Bellows, of Wilton, N. H.

4. Hymn—(*Written for the occasion.*)

Eternal God, thine endless years
Know not the shadow of a change;
While our brief days for ever see
Strange scenes give way to scenes more strange.

But every change thy mercy shows—
Thy goodness, unexhausted wealth;
In each we see thy loving hand,
That still supplies our life and health.

We bless the providence that led
Our father to this lovely spot;
That shielded him from savage foes,
And filled with good his earthly lot.

We pray the fathers' God to bless
The children, wheresoe'er they roam;
To shield them from their hidden foes,
And lead them to a heavenly home.

Help us to fill our father's place;
Like him to be in all things true
Toward men on earth, toward Christ in heaven,
And thine be praises ever new.

T. H.

5. Benediction.

[*At the Town-Hall.*]

6. Historical Address, by Rev. H. W. Bellows, D.D., of New-York.

7. Hymn—(*Written for the occasion.*)

The God who plants the forest oak,
Firm in its native soil;
The God who made that river flow,
Without man's thought or toil;

He planted in the forest, men;
He gave them strength of will;
They came because He called them here
His purpose to fulfill.

They did his work—lived lives of truth—
Were honest, simple, brave;
Unconscious that they founded thus
The race and home we love.

As grows the oak, with growing years
They grew from strength to strength;
As flows that stream, with constant flow,
They ever onward went.

Their branches spread, their arms reached wide,
And sheltered many there;
The seed they sowed, the house they reared,
Were blessed as if by prayer.

It is not then to praise our sires,
But offer thanks to God,
That we this monument have raised,
Above their hallowed sod.

To God we offer thanks, and pray
That now and evermore,
Whene'er our lips repeat their name,
His mercy we adore.

And while the forest sounds a dirge,
And river murmurs on,
The good men's name shall oft be spoke,
By father down to son.

K.

8. Prayer, by Rev. Thomas Hill, of Waltham, Mass.

[*Collation.*]

9. ODE—(*Written for the occasion.*)

Kindred and friends, to-day we meet,
And heart and hand responsive greet;
Our thought and purpose still the same—
Honor give to an honored name.
Hither, from far and near we come,
And all shall have "a welcome home."

What though the prairies of the West
Show richer plains, in verdure dressed,
Or Southern breezes milder blow;
A dearer charm the heart can know.
Hither, from far and near we come,
And all shall have "a welcome home."

Our father's gift, this valley fair,
Won by his toil and patient care,
With circling hills that round it stand,
The guardians of the favored land.
Hither, from far and near we come,
To seek and find "a welcome home."

Youth, and old age, and manhood's prime,
Meet childhood's gay and joyous time;
Each wearying care cast far away,
Let love and gladness rule to-day.
Bound by one kindred tie we come,
And all have found "a welcome home."

10. ADDRESSES.

11. ODE—(*Written for the occasion.*)

No costly column, reared to mark
The spot where our forefather lay,
Was needed to preserve his name,
And keep oblivion from its prey.

We did not fear lest he should be
Forgottěn in the lapse of years;
Since all the thriving scene around
His lasting monument appears.

We raised that stone to tell the world
Our own deep reverence for his name—
Our gratitude for what he was—
Our earnest wish to be the same.

His virtues in our lives we'll show,
Our children teach to do the same;
Unworthy sons of such a sire
Shall on that marble read their shame.

T. H.

12. ADDRESSES.

13. ODE—(*Written for the occasion.*)

TUNE, "AULD LANG SYNE."

Come, friends and brothers, kinsmen all,
From mountain, plain, and sea,
Come, gather fast at nature's call,
To keep our Jubilee.
This day a monument we build
To him who won the soil,
Where Walpole town now stands, well filled
With fruits of manly toil.

The Indian foe assailed his path,
Wild beasts in ambush lay;
He recked not of their skill and wrath,
But onward held his way.
Fair woman, too, his cause to aid,
Assisted in the strife;
And thus were these foundations laid,
The work of man and wife.

Heroic heart! we honor thee
For all thy toil and pain;
That danger, exile, thou didst bear,
That we a home might gain;
For now along these peaceful vales
We hear the voice of song,
While ancient annals tell the tales
Of conflicts fierce and long.

From him, the fearless, true, and strong,
We date our race and birth,
While many generations throng
To celebrate his worth.

United, firm in heart and hand
Oh! let our race be found,
For Liberty and Truth to stand
On our dear native ground.

Perhaps our ancestor looks down
Upon this scene to-day,
And blesses God, in conscious thought,
For all we do and say.
Perhaps—we know not how it is—
That spirits walk the earth,
And minister to human bliss,
By power of heavenly birth.

Our fathers' graves, the dear old men!
So firm, and wise, and true,
Let's drop a tear upon their sod,
And emulate them too;
Peaceful their ashes sleep beneath
These mounds that near us lie;
May we, like them, to earth bequeath
A name that will not die.

J. N. B.

THE COLLATION.

We give below a report of the toasts and remarks at the collation in the Town-Hall.

At the table, the following preliminary remarks were made by B. B. Grant, Chairman:

My Friends: Now that you will feel, perhaps, less impatient than you would have done a half-hour ago, I will say a few words. Not belonging to the talking branch of the family, I shall not attempt a speech. I will, however, repeat our welcome. As Chairman of the Committee, which has had charge of erecting the monument to our honored ancestor, I find that it falls to me to speak this word to you. That word "welcome" is always a pleasant word to repeat, but especially pleasant is it when it extends to so many friends and kindred, and comes from warm hearts; for I speak on this occasion, not for myself alone; I speak in behalf of those whose home is still here where our father dwelt. They reach out a hand to you who have come from other homes. They, each one and all, welcome you, and surely this day there should be warm hearts and cordial hands, when we remember the heart and the hand of him whose name we repeat, Benjamin Bellows—Colonel Benjamin Bellows, one of nature's noblemen, commanding in person, and greatly distinguished for his noble deeds, as well as for his generous hospitality; may the present and future descendants, aye and those who may in any way become connected with them, imitate his example.

I congratulate all concerned upon the happy conclusion of this undertaking, upon the ready response for pecuniary aid, upon the strong family feeling which has been called out; for, believe me, I am in possession, from contributors, of many warm and patriotic letters. Finally, I congratulate you upon this happy meeting, around, as it were, the old family table. Many of you have been long absent from each other, while many doubtless will date the commencement of their acquaintance from this day and occasion. I have heretofore, in letters addressed to some of our cousins, intimated that a brief account of the descendants of Colonel Bellows, together with some other facts, would be prepared for distribution at this time. I have, however, been unable as yet to gather the requisite information, but flatter myself that the leisure of the coming winter will enable me to do so, in which event copies shall be transmitted to the numerous families.

After the remarks of Mr. Grant, the Ode of Welcome was sung. Then followed the reading of a series of toasts, with biographical remarks prefixed, presenting the names of the sons and daughters of Colonel Bellows in the order of their birth.

The memory of Colonel Benjamin Bellows, the Founder of Walpole: his portrait has just been presented to you.

This toast was responded to by Francis Bellows Knapp, of Walpole, as follows:

In memory of those whose eminent genius, virtues, or public services were held worthy of especial honor, the ancient Greeks raised statues and monuments. They told their history not in letters alone, but in brass and stone. The temples they built to their gods were consecrated by placing there the living forms, as it were, of their law-givers, statesmen, and sages. Nor in their temples only did they raise these statues, but in the places of more public resort; thus in their daily walks and daily business, the great and good men of former days were present with them still. "The past" to them, it has been well said, "lived and breathed anew." Thus have we sought this day, in the honors paid to the past, to keep fresh and glowing in our memories the virtues of our ancestors, that they also to us may be ever-living and present.

In the history of the Puritans, that noble, stern, stout-hearted race, who, leaving their native homes, landed on the bleak coasts of New-England, amid hardships and sufferings, unprotected and unseen, save by that God for whose service they had left their friends and homes; who reared on the rock of Plymouth their first altar, and in faith and prayer kindled thereon those fires of liberty and religion, in that race, we may find many of those same elements of character, the same fearlessness and fortitude, the same high resolve and heroic courage, and devotion to that noble work for which they had been chosen; the same sacrificing, martyr-like spirit, and invincible will; the same calm, practical wisdom, and warm and deep affections; the same Christian faith, the same Christian love—many of which elements we find in that man who felled those forests, and planted these homes. Honor, then, to the memory of Colonel Benjamin Bellows, the devout, strong, bold-minded, whole-souled, God-fearing, truth-loving man, the Founder of our town and father of our race. I have often been struck with what an English historian has said of those men who, in the days of Cromwell, for wisdom and valor stood first and foremost: "If they were unacquainted," he says, "with the works of philosophers and poets, they were deeply read in the oracles of God. If their names were not found in the register of heralds, they felt assured they were recorded in the book of life. On the rich and eloquent, on nobles and priests, they looked down with contempt; for they esteemed themselves rich in a more precious treasure, and eloquent in a more sublime language; nobles by the right of an earlier creation, and priests by the imposition of a mightier hand."

These were the ancestors of our New-England fathers. Nerved and emboldened with the inspiration that comes from such a parentage, their sons labored on, raising in strength and beauty that structure, whose foundations the Pilgrims laid.

If it be deemed not out of place here, I would like to say a word in memory of that well-nigh forgotten race, whose ancient dwelling-place was our New-England valleys; for, I believe, were our ancestor here to-day, from his generous heart he would say, Friends, turn from me a while, and speak a word of those whom my heart honored, even if nature made them my foes. There are bright pages even in their bloody record. We have been wont from childhood to regard the Indian in no other light than as cruel and ferocious, with but few of those many virtues that are the adornment and boast of civilized life. All their high, heroic acts, their manly struggle in defense of their rights, their courage in the battle-field, their wisdom at the council-fire, are mostly forgotten, or if ever recalled, present to the imagination scenes of terror, the reeking tomahawk and scalping-knife. But are these altogether true? are there no redeeming virtues in him? nothing that calls for and claims our sympathy? I said there was a bright page even in their history; look for a moment at their spiritual belief; to me there is in it much that is beautiful, well-nigh sacred. Most nations, even in their childhood, though trusting alone to the suggestions and teachings of nature, and the desires and promptings that are born in every human soul, seem to have caught some conception of a spiritual world, of spiritual being; it is seen in the bold, rude, and oftentimes sublime legends of the Northmen; in those strange, mystic, imaginative fables of the East; in the fertile, poetical, and polished mythology of the Greek. The Red-man, too, had his legends as bold, grand, and poetical as Scandanavian or Greek. All the works of God to him were governed by the power, filled with the presence, and vocal with the music of guardian and celestial spirits. Mountain, valley, and hill-side, he believed, were not the dwelling-place of the Red-man alone; to him the soft light resting on the gentle lake was the smile of the Great Spirit; the winds that swept and swayed the great forests, his breath; and the thunder of the mighty cataract, his voice; the setting sun, rich in golden light, had for him its parting benediction.

The same imagination that so invested and adorned outward nature, had built for him a paradise of its own, far more beautiful than that pictured in the dreams of Mecca's prophet, where white-robed houris beckoned the dying warrior to its gates, promising, for delight and reward, indolence and voluptuousness for ever. In the South-west, the land of the Great Spirit, there the Indian believed that at last his kindred and tribe should be gathered to find wider hunting-grounds and happier homes.

But to return. Had we time, we should like to draw the picture, if but in faint and fading colors, that seems to stand out from the past, so living and life-like before us; the picture, we say, of the old age of our Founder. The very naming of those words, "old age," sounds sweet and well-nigh sacred to the ear of many a one. Are they not fragrant words, linked in with early thoughts and pleasant memories? Are they not, too, words of encouragement and promise? To the young, filled and freighted with joy and hope, that future when his dreams shall be realized and his prayers answered, or, if his pilgrimage should prove weary and sore, as perchance it may, will they not be to him as the oasis in the desert of his life, where, for a while, resting from his toil, he may lay down his burden, brush the dust from off his sandals, and drinking from the fountain which ever flows there, rise up, ready to go on his way with fresh strength and new resolves?

Twenty-six years had passed since that day when our ancestor, in the prime of manhood, came to his wilderness-home—years crowded with stirring and thrilling events. And now in ripe age, having accomplished the work given him to do, having fulfilled the mission he had been chosen to perform, in Christian fortitude and with Christian trust he calmly awaited the summons he knew must soon come, and which he was prepared to meet. "There be of them that have left a name behind, that their praises might be reported; merciful men, whose righteousness shall not be forgotten; their seed shall remain for ever, and their glory shall not be blotted out. Their bodies are buried in peace, but their name liveth for ever more."

May yonder monument, with its firm base, its sculptured sides, and its fair shaft, stand for many, many years, emblem and memorial of him, whom we, his children, have gathered here this day to honor. In conclusion, allow me to offer this sentiment: May our race be numbered among those whose high privilege it is to be enabled to hand down, from generation to generation, an unsullied name, and the record of lives, enriched and consecrated by wise and virtuous deeds. "For the memorial of virtue is immortal; when it is present, men take example of it; when it is gone, they desire it; it weareth a crown, and triumpheth for ever."

I. The toast-master then said: Having honored the trunk, we will now call your attention to the ten principal branches of the family tree.

Abigail, the first child, the fondling of her father's heart, was beautiful and lovely, of sweet temper and engaging manners, intelligent and good. When at school at Northampton, in the twentieth year of her age, she left this earthly scene, and took her upward flight.

"The memory of Abigail, the first child of the Founder of this town: the fairest, earliest-blown flower in Walpole was consecrated an offering to heaven."

II. The second child was of small size, but of a bright mind and keen wit. He loved social intercourse, and was the life of it. Abounding in humor and ingenious repartee, he delighted the young, and made the aged throw off their gravity. The spirit of avarice never got hold of him, and its meanness never degraded him. Tranquillity and freedom from care were his ruling passion.

"The memory of Peter, the first son:

"Some place their bliss in action, some in ease;
Those call it pleasure, and contentment these."

III. The second son commanded great respect by his personal appearance, even where the weight of his character was not known. An unaffected suavity and politeness conciliated esteem and affection. His integrity and veracity were unimpeachable. Avarice never approached him. He found greater pleasure in giving than in accumulating. His hospitality, like that of his father, was limited only by the opportunities of exercising it. His friendship was lasting. The purity of his character defied suspicion. His political views were formed under Washington influences. He was a nobleman, with republican principles. He had wisdom to aid in the councils of the country; and courage and skill to fight her battles.

"The memory of General Benjamin Bellows: Nature stamped him with her imperial signet, 'to give the world assurance of a man.'"

This last sentiment was responded to by Edward Bellows Grant, of Boston, as follows:

I am a lineal descendant from him whose memory we are assembled to celebrate.

Colonel Benjamin Bellows was my great-grandfather on my mother's side, and my great-great-grandfather on my father's side. His second son, General Benjamin Bellows, was my great-grandfather on my father's side. The orator of the day has informed us of his services and virtues. He was beloved and respected for his hospitality and intelligence, his humanity and his honesty; traits that constitute a noble legacy, which all must desire to bequeath to their posterity.

My father's remembrance of the General must obviously be indistinct, as he was but six years of age at the time of his grandfather's decease. However, he well recollects sitting upon the knee of a kind and indulgent old man, of great courtliness and dignity of manner, and scrupulous nicety in dress. He remembers being summoned to the side of his grandfather's death-bed, and his recollections are most vivid of the great length of the procession that followed the remains of the worthy old patriot and public servant to their last resting-place.

My father recollects the pipe-tongs of polished steel, to which allusion has been made, and which I am glad to learn are in the possession of one of the General's granddaughters. The belt of wampum, to which reference has also been made, is in the possession of one of his grandsons.

The erection of the cenotaph we have this day consecrated in yonder cemetery, leads the mind back to that comparatively remote period, 1752, when this town received its charter.

It is a noble feeling in our nature that prompts us to reverence antiquity; and it seems fitting in this age of progress, perhaps too rapid, when "footprints on the sands of time" are so quickly obliterated, that we should occasionally pause to testify our appreciation of the good and great who have preceded us, by the erection of permanent memorials of their services or their virtues.

These monuments, called into existence by hearts affectionate and grateful, serve as landmarks, indicating the progress of civilization, and its concomitant arts.

They are also beacons, to guide in kindred paths of rectitude the feet of those, the memory of whose ancestors yet lives, not only in marble, but in the hearts of grateful descendants.

Such testimonials are peculiarly due to those whose strong arms conquered for their children this land, now adorned by civilization and the arts of peace. This town has had a chartered existence for more than one hundred years. But little more than a century ago, these hills and valleys had never been trodden by the foot of the Anglo-Saxon.

Since that time what changes have taken place!

New-Hampshire, then included within the boundaries of Massachusetts, was an almost unbroken wilderness, tenanted by wild beasts, and Indians scarcely less savage.

Now, behold an endless landscape of cultivated fields, tilled by intelligent and Christian men.

Then, the most rapid mode of travel was on horseback; Boston was four days journey hence.

Now, the enterprise of the descendants of the hardy pioneers has levelled the hills and valleys, and, over a smooth and even road, our transit is so rapid, that in effect we are within the suburbs of that metropolis.

Boston then contained but 14,574 inhabitants, scattered over the peninsula, the houses for the most part being slight structures of wood.

Now, its busy streets crowded with a population of 150,000, its churches and schools of learning, the costly residences of its millionaires, its warehouses of enduring granite, its wharves crowded with shipping, its railroads, those iron veins through which life is diffused throughout the commonwealth; and last, and best of all, its noble philanthropists, foremost in every good work, all tell of progress.

Our country, then a feeble province, contained but little more than a million of people, under the sway of George II. of England.

Now, a gigantic empire, whose shores are washed by two mighty oceans, with a population of 25,000,000 of happy and self-governing people, rivaling the foremost powers of Christendom in intelligence, wealth, and power. These hills, once echoing to the sound of the fierce war-whoop, now give back, in a thousand notes, the challenge of the locomotive, that iron emblem of the age, and potent instrument of civilization, which opens to the hand of industry broad territories hitherto unsubdued. The timid deer, then undisturbed by man, their deadliest enemy, have given place to herds more noble, and better fitted to the service of man, their master.

The light canoe, that once stole like a shadow over the glassy bosoms of our lakes and rivers, or danced upon the ocean waves around our rocky headlands, has disappeared; and the huge leviathan, with ribs of oak and lungs of fire, now bears our flag in honor to the uttermost parts of the sea.

The fierce lightning, once striking terror to the heart of the superstitious savage; now, obedient to man, has become his willing and fleetest messenger.

Here and there a towering pine and wide-spreading oak remain, silent witnesses of all these changes.

Those who wrought these wonders have, for the most part, been gathered to their kindred dust; but let us hope that their dauntless spirits yet live in the bosoms of worthy children, and when the sands of another century shall have run out, may our posterity be the chroniclers of changes still more memorable for Christian progress.

It is meet that we should this day commune, not only with the past and the present, but with the future. Let us, therefore, turn our feeble visions onward, and attempt to pierce the veil that hides that future.

If one hundred years have wrought such changes, what may we not hope of the coming century?

In the language of the giant of our time, upon a somewhat similar occasion: "We can win no laurels in a war for independence. Earlier and worthier hands have gathered them all. Nor are there places for us by the side of Solon and Alfred, and other founders of states. Our fathers have filled them. But there remains to us a great duty of defense and preservation, and there is opened to us, also, a noble pursuit, to which the spirit of the times strongly invites us. Our proper business is improvement. Let our age be an age of improvement. In a day of peace, let us advance the arts of peace and the works of peace. Let us develop the resources of the land, call forth its powers, build up its institutions, promote all its great interests, and see whether we, also, in our day and generation, may not perform something worthy to be remembered."

He who uttered these sentiments has gone to join the good and the great who preceded him.

Death cuts off here and there a fainting straggler, but new names are added to the roll, and the grand army of life, under other leaders, marches on to fresh conquests.

Yonder river, its particles all changed, yet rolls its endless tide as in those elder days; its fertilizing influences still felt in the "soft-falling snow and the diffusive rain," under the same ceaseless law of nature that a kind Providence established ages and ages ago; and thus it will roll on for ever.

But let us profit by the teaching of one of New-Hampshire's noblest sons.

May the work given us to do be as faithfully performed as was that of our ancestors. May our children and children's children progress in civilization and Christianity, until, in God's good time, sin and injustice in this broad land shall find no abiding-place.

Our opportunities are far greater than were those of our ancestors. Every hill-side, every valley is studded with temples dedicated to religion, to education, to progress.

The free press, one of the mightiest, perhaps the most mighty engine of civilization, is daily scattering broadcast over the land, seeds of truth and intelligence that must blossom and bring forth a noble harvest.

In 1754, there were but ten newspapers published in the provinces; now, 2526 periodical publications, with an annual circulation of 426,409,978 copies, and 10,199 libraries, containing 3,753,964 volumes, combine to shed the light of intelligence upon every subject in which humanity is interested.

And when another century is numbered; when, by the blessing of God, this country shall contain within its borders 200,000,000 of Christians, may the sun, from the rising to the going down thereof, shine upon a nation of freemen; freemen in every sense of that noble word, living under one happy government, the stability of which is guaranteed by the character of its Christian population.

It is not in a day that the wilderness is to be subdued; but from the past learn what the future may be.

As the country progresses in wealth, in intelligence and refinement, the ennobling pursuit of agriculture will dot the broad bosom of the land with the residences of gentlemen, who will bring to their aid all the appliances of wealth, of taste, and of science for its cultivation and adornment.

This beautiful valley, these noble hills, from river-side to mountain-top, will bloom like a garden.

The irresistible influence of Christianity, of education, and of commerce will overthrow the already crumbling walls that imprison one third of the human race in China and Japan. Our posterity will extend the right-hand of fellowship to enfranchised millions in Europe. The foul blots that disfigure our land will be effaced; the evils that exist in our time, numbered with things that are past.

Then, in truth, there will be "no north, no south, no east, no west;" but one universal brotherhood of nations, with one aim and one end—the happiness of humanity. Thus will the purposes of an all-wise Father be accomplished.

IV. The third son had a manly and commanding bearing. His countenance had no common-place expression. He had a quickness of perception, soundness of judgment, and a penetrating foresight. Shrewd and calculating, his success in business was conspicuous. He accumulated safely, and in his family expended liberally. He was punctual and exact in the fulfillment of his promises, and brought others up to the same standard. The careless, slack, or lazy found with him neither sympathy nor indulgence. His determined energy was felt in whatever he engaged. His virtues and talents gained esteem and commanded respect.

"The memory of Col. John Bellows, the third son. 'The hand of the diligent maketh rich.' 'He who causes two spears of grass to grow where only one grew before, is a benefactor to mankind.'"

Mr. S. A. Millard, of Troy, N. Y., responded to this sentiment as follows:

"Mr. Chairman: You call upon me to respond to the sentiment in behalf of Colonel John Bellows. I feel, sir, both surprised and complimented; surprised at being called upon out of the midst of this large circle of his descendants—and complimented that you should do so without any kind of previous intimation.

"But, sir, upon the principle (which serves me well in this case) that man and wife are one, I, too, am a descendant of that estimable man. A position, sir, I am this day proud to maintain.

"And how well is this meeting, this gathering of generous offspring, calculated both to revive the memory of the departed ancestor, and incite the children to emulate his noble deeds! These kinds of family-gatherings, sir, have been commented upon by some as reünions of vanity; but I am persuaded that such strictures have only proceeded from those unfortunate descendants who had no ancestral fame to cherish.

"Rather than be deterred, then, by such envious criticisms, we will in pity forgive the assailant, and pray that he himself may constitute the head of a stock worthy of lineal remembrance.

"Sir, this is a beautiful scene. It is a gladdening sight to cast the eye around upon the happy faces of so many kindred here assembled to do honor to a worthy house. And what emotion of the human heart is more admirable, or affords better evidence of a good *heart*, than gratitude; and that kind of venerating gratitude, too, that has this day brought together, from various and distant parts of this broad land, so many grateful descendants, to join in one common anthem of gratitude at the grave of him whose memory we this day celebrate. There are none here, sir, but true gratitudinarians—none others come on occasions like this. And it is a justifiable pride we take to-day in extolling our great-grandparent. It incites to good deeds, and reminds us what we owe to the maintenance of our hereditary fame. Of the noble characteristics of that grand-parent it does not become me to speak. They have been portrayed by a master's hand, and made to shine out in manly brightness. His uncommon hospitality, so much spoken of, is here admirably typified in the generous spread of these clustering tables, to which we have just paid such good heed. I am convinced that hospitality is clearly a prominent characteristic of the Bellows family, both in giving and receiving.

"But of the succeeding generations of that good man, I may with confidence speak. It has been my blessed lot to be connected with one, and to, have formed most agreeable association with numerous of her kin; and that *one* was worthy of her great grandsire, whatever may have been his good qualities; and although we are here met to commemorate the deeds of our ancestors in the male line, I can not forbear the suggestion that if there is any thing in the idea, and I believe there is much, that we owe our traits of character mainly to our mothers, then there must have been many good mothers linked to these families of Bellowses.

"You, however, ask me to speak of Colonel John. What shall I say? What could I say that would more redound to his honor and glory, than that the great strength of the moral characteristics of Colonel John, so graphically delineated by the orator this day, are still sternly and sweetly illustrated in the present generation. My own wife, on whose account I am here on this occasion, and in whose behalf I am called upon to speak, was a noble among the noblest. What a wife! what a mother! Pardon this obtrusive tear. It is not for her, but for mine and her children's loss, it is shed."

V. The fourth son was a man of commanding person and dignified manners; of enlarged benevolence and humanity; much loved and confided in for his rectitude, and often referred to for the soundness of his judgment and the weight of his character. As a revolutionary patriot he was ardent and active. He was a faithful and tender husband and an affectionate father. "The elements were so kindly mixt in him," that neither malice, envy, or ill-nature ever found even a transient entrance into his heart. He was of that sensitive temperament which belongs to a poetic love of the beauty and harmony of nature, and of great susceptibility to what is intellectually and morally sublime. It was because of this sensitive temperament that he received so great a shock from misfortune as to bring a lasting cloud over his intellectual vision.

"The memory of Col. Joseph Bellows. 'The pure in heart shall see God.'"

This sentiment was responded to by Rev. John N. Bellows, of Wilton, New-Hampshire. We regret not to have a copy of the appropriate and beautiful remarks which he made.

VI. The second daughter was a lady of great worth. When young, she was the observed of all observers, and "cynosure of neighboring eyes." She was a woman of quick perceptions and clear judgment, of great cheerfulness of temper and playful wit, a thorough and practical housewife, and a delightful companion to the old and the young; for, although she lived to be more than eighty years of age, her heart never lost any of its warmth or freshness. From natural temperament and religious influence, she was social, kind, benevolent, charitable in her opinions, compassionate and forgiving.

"The memory of Abigail Richardson. It lies embalmed in the hearts of all who knew her."

Dr. Morse, of Walpole, responded to this toast as follows:

Mr. Chairman: I have been honored with an invitation to this family gathering, to attend as "family physician," and although there is no apparent call for any prescriptions for the present company, still it is a singular fact that I have prescribed for seven of the children of Colonel Benjamin Bellows, who lived in this town more than one hundred years ago.

But, sir, I am particularly caused to speak at this time, because no one else has responded to "the memory of Mrs. Abigail Richardson." Why, it would be doing injustice to her memory, as well as to this joyous gathering, to suffer the name of such a repository of fun, wit, and humor to pass in silence. Those who knew her best can recollect the thousand instances in which the faces of her friendly circles were mellowed and made the happier by her pleasant remarks. The anecdote related by the orator, of her threatening to bury her husband in the ash-hole, was one of her most laughable and ludicrous hits, that never can be repeated without producing violent convulsions of the ribs and diaphragm. Even in her childhood, it was "Naby Bellows" that "required two to keep her from making fun in meeting-time."

And the same humor, during her whole life, was her prevailing complaint, which, on all occasions and in all weather, would be constantly breaking out, particularly about the mouth, and which the abstemious diet of bread and milk, which I prescribed, had no power to cure.

Mr. Charles Bellows, of Northumberland, New-Hampshire, added some appropriate words in connection with this toast.

VII. The fifth son was of great stature and remarkable strength, and of an easy and kind temper. The restless spirit of ambition never possessed him, or involved him in its complicated intrigues. He never entered the list of competitors for wealth or glory.

"The memory of Theodore Bellows. The Sampson of the family, who never had his locks shorn by a Delilah, or had any quarrel with Philistines, or was compelled to grind in a prison."

VIII. The sixth son was a person extensively known, and wherever known, loved and respected. Much employed in offices of private trust, his honesty was proverbial, his veracity was unquestionable, his judgment was never blinded or perverted by strong passions. He was, in all matters referred to him, just as Aristides. His patriotism was not ephemeral, but a permanent principle and an unchangeable feeling. His integrity, like that of Fabricius, was incorruptible by offers of wealth or power. As a lover of improvements, his purse was opened liberally. A friend of good institutions, he was always generous in support of them. In public offices, he commanded confidence and respect. Popularity *followed* him. *Benevolence* was the most striking trait in his character. With him it was not only a principle, but an innate warmth of heart. The needy never carried away an empty bag from his granary. He was the friend of humanity, and the benefactor of the destitute.

"The memory of Thomas Bellows: Always a useful, exemplary, and honorable man. 'The memory of the just is blessed.'"

Mr. Thomas Bellows, of Walpole, followed this mention of his father, with brief but appropriate remarks.

IX. The third daughter was a lady of commanding person and dignified manners. Her mind had great strength and clearness. Her conversation was marked by argument and seriousness. Her courage was heroic. She never set up new theories on the rights of woman, but with readiness and fidelity performed all the duties which God and nature taught her belonged to the good wife, tender mother, and to an exemplary member of society. She lived and died an earnest and devout Christian.

"The memory of Mary Kinsley: 'Blessed are the dead that die in the Lord.'"

Mr. Thomas Bellows made a brief response to this toast, bearing testimony to its truth and justice, and regretting that the orator of the day had not paid more attention to the ladies of the family in his address.

Rev. H. W. Bellows begged pardon for occupying any further portion of the time, but he could not fail to acknowledge the justice of the friendly rebuke which his cousin, Mr. Thomas Bellows, (doubtless to cover his own notorious delinquencies,) had given him for not devoting more time to the ladies of the family in the address of the day. He was particularly glad to have his shortcomings made up by the notice which their memories had just received. Nothing but absolute want of time could excuse the absence of the full tributes which were due to the honored mothers of our race. To them we were indebted for services, the first to be needed and the last to be commemorated; indebted for whatever had given comfort, order, thrift, and refinement to the homes in which our fathers had lived and we were born; services to which those homes owed a large part of their prosperity and all their happiness. One anecdote connected with the character of Mrs. General Bellows, of whom his own father had always spoken with affectionate reverence, he could not forbear to name here. After her husband's death, the Judges of the County Court, in honor of his worthy memory, offered her the nomination of a candidate for the lucrative office of Register of Deeds, for which her own son was understood to be a wishful expectant, and to which, of course, she had every inducement of affection and interest to promote him. Mr. Abel Bellows, then just beginning life, a member of an unprosperous branch of the family, also wanted the office, and it lay in her power to give it to her nephew or to her only son. She quickly decided it. "Caleb," said she, "is well off, and has enough for his good; Abel needs it, and I recommend him to the appointment." The judges gave it to his uncle, and the thousand dollars he made in one year's occupancy of the office—for party politics ousted him after that period—was, he had heard him say, the foundation of his fortune. Was not this a noble woman?

We were indebted, moreover, to the excellency and attractiveness of the ladies of the family, for some of the most valuable acquisitions of their social circle; for some how, instead of their girls marrying *on* to other families, they had usually married their husbands *on* to theirs. He would not say how the husbands may have fared in the hands of such strong characters; but here was his venerable Uncle Knapp, one of the most valuable spoils of their victorious women, who looks and lasts like one not suffering severely from ill-treatment. Some of their most valued guests on this occasion were here in the right of their wives, and they were proud to see what their ladies had achieved by conquest for the honor and enrichment of the family. He trusted that more and more their sisters and daughters would bring their husbands home to Walpole, and that it would be a part of every future marriage contract in this extraordinary family, that as the spoils belong to the victors, so the ladies own the husbands, and bring them to the homestead, not the husbands the wives, as in ordinary families, where the rule is properly enough reversed.

X. The seventh son was a man of strong mind and inflexible integrity; liberal and just. His promise was a bond which was never forfeited. When intrusted with a secret, no one could find the key or pick the lock which secured it. He despised frippery and ostentation; was firm in his resolves, and persevering in his purposes. His house offered a generous board and a hearty welcome. The love of notoriety never allured him. Political office he never sought or desired. He lived and died a private, a useful, intelligent citizen.

"The memory of Josiah Bellows, youngest son of the Founder of Walpole: his tombstone may say,

'What few vain marbles can;
Here lies an honest man.'"

Mr. William Bellows, of Walpole, spoke in substance, as follows:

Mr. Chairman and Friends: It is painful to me to attempt a response to the sentiment just offered, so complimentary to the head of our branch of the family; conscious as I am that I shall do it feebly. The history of his life proves that our progenitor, the founder of this town, was no ordinary man. It indicated strong judgment, made effective by energy of will, and directed by noble sentiments. It showed him hospitable, just, and conscientious, responding generously to all public and private claims.

My occupation has made me familiar with the influence of "blood" in the animal races, having seen, in numerous instances, the distinguishing characteristics of a noble sire, transmitted from generation to generation; and it is with much pleasure that I observe that the branches of our family tree bear the same fruit as did the original stock. The unanimity with which the call for money to erect this monument was answered, and the assembling of so many distant branches to-day, answers the inquiry in the address, "If you ever knew a Bellows to be sordidly mean."

The head of our branch of the family, it is unnecessary for me to say, was just, wise, and liberal, and the remembrance of the baskets of broken meats which daily blessed the needy at his door, is among the earliest recollections of my boyhood.

The devotion, judgment, and energy manifested by the Chairman of your Committee, in completing the undertaking, proves that the strong points in the family character are not obliterated.

The Chairman here called upon Jacob N. Knapp, Esq., as the author of the regular toasts, and desired him to speak for himself.

Mr. Knapp spoke as follows:

I am called upon for a sentiment. As, in consequence of great age, I stand near the confines of both worlds, and can hardly be said to belong to either, my words will be few.

If I should speak of the present condition, the prospects, and probable future extent of the family name, connections, and character, the subject would last much longer than my strength. If I should speak of those who have been called to leave us, I should be in danger of opening afresh the deep fountains of sorrow. But there is one grave which I can not pass in silence; my heart demands an utterance. In that grave rest the remains of a gifted son of the family and name. Many of you remember his commanding person and manly bearing. His mind was of a high order. He seized subjects with a strong intellectual grasp. Truth had in him a champion. Falsehood was quickly stripped of its counterfeit robes, and its deformity exposed. Nature formed him for an orator and statesman. In addition to the properties just named, he had an ardent temperament, a strongly-marked countenance, good memory, brilliant imagination, a strong, deep, well-toned voice, and graceful gesture. He was a well-read lawyer, and acquainted with the civil and political history of our country; and had at his command playful humor, stinging sarcasm, and keen-edged satire. Had he lived, the halls of Congress would, before this time, have listened to his eloquence, and the confidence of the public have been secured by his integrity and firmness.

Just as he entered on the stage, for a life of usefulness, when in the western wilds, far from any habitation, and in the discharge of an arduous professional duty, the curtain of life dropped, and concealed him from our view.

His grave is solitary. No friends or kindred lie near him. The winds, yes, the *pitying* winds of heaven, as they breathe among the trees of the dark western forests, mourn the sudden fall, and continually, night and day, sing a requiem over the early grave of Edward Stearns Bellows, a twin-brother by birth, and in spirit, to the gifted orator of the day.

> "The ways of heaven are dark and intricate,
> Puzzled in mazes, and perplexed in *seeming* errors.
> Holy father, not our will, but thine be done."

I turn from the dead to the living; from those never to be forgotten to you present, assembled to consecrate a monumental memorial to your ancestor. I see among you representatives from every useful and honorable pursuit; substantial farmers, the foundation stones of the temple of American liberty; artisans ready to repair any dilapidations in the walls of the edifice, and to add to its ornaments; enterprising merchants, who bring into it riches and luxuries from every region; physicians of skill and celebrity; counsellors-at-law, the eloquent advocates of justice; ministers of religion, consecrated to purity and holiness, and to invoking the mercies and blessings of heaven; wise, discreet, and honorable matrons, with sons whom they are training to become pillars of our republic, also with fair, well-educated, and accomplished daughters, polished after the similitude of a palace; and many children of tender age, the inestimable family jewels—a great gathering round the ancient family hearth-stone.

This convention will introduce a new epoch in the family circle. Hereafter we shall date not only from the founding of Walpole, but from this era of fraternal affections renewed, sympathies deepened, friendships confirmed, pride gratified, pleasant introductions made, generous emulations kindled, and aspiring resolves silently formed by many individuals to be, in merit and honorable distinction, not *behind* the *foremost.*

I offer you a sentiment:

"The eulogist, local historian, and eloquent orator of the day; of the family tree a vigorous branch, continually producing a rich variety of intellectual fruit of great beauty and delicious flavor."

Rev. H. W. Bellows said, he had taken a vow of silence, but must break it to respond to the delicate and touching speech, in which his venerable Uncle, the teacher of his youth, the example of his manhood, and the revered and delightful companion of his leisure, had embalmed the character of his twin-brother Edward, now dead for eighteen years, but living in all the freshness of his genius and the proud promise of his nature, in his own grieved and ever-regretful heart. Generous and exalted as the tribute was, which his uncle, who thoroughly knew his brother, had just paid to his memory, he felt bound to say, that it did not exceed the sober deserts of its subject. Among all the young men of high talents and noble qualities he had had the happiness to know, he had yet met no peer of his brother. Splendid in natural endowments, both of person and intellect, exalted in ambition, and made to govern and to teach, his sudden death deprived his family and his country of a jewel of the purest water, deprived him of an immeasurable blessing, a companion in mind and heart, shaped to him in the very womb, and fulfilling every year higher and better conditions of true friendship and sympathy. Long might the venerable man who taught them both, survive to receive their gratitude, and to confer his benedictions. He could ask no tenderer or more copious eulogist were he in his own grave. His uncle's eulogy did not wait for his departure, or they might well wish for their own sakes that it should never be spoken.

The following toast was then offered by Mr. Francis B. Knapp:

"The early ministers of Walpole: Watchmen on the towers of our Zion."

This was responded to by Rev. W. P. Tilden, of Walpole:

Mr. Tilden, in responding to the call, said in substance: That he was happy in being present, as an invited guest, to share in the pleasure and hospitalities of this occasion. But as the hour was late; as they had already heard so much, and were still anticipating another meeting in the evening, of a somewhat different character, when they could take each other by the hand, and talk face to face in a still more familiar and social manner; therefore, he would not attempt to say what, under other circumstances, he should have been happy to have said, of the early ministers of Walpole.

He would offer instead the following sentiment:

"The present collection of *Bellows:* May they never lend their powers to fan an unhallowed flame; but kindle only such fires as warm and purify, while they remember the beautiful motto of their fathers, 'All from above.'"

After Mr. Tilden had spoken, Rev. H. W. Bellows read the following letter from Rev. F. N. Knapp, of Brookline, Massachusetts:

"BROOKLINE, Mass., Oct. 11, 1854.

"FRIENDS AND KINSMEN: I can not join you in person; sickness prevents; but my heart is with you to-day. Full of joy, and happy as a 'family gathering' may be, I know that it always adds even to that happiness to receive, after all are seated at the table, a message from an absent son, though that message contain nothing more than these words: 'I want to be with you; my thoughts and affections are there. God bless you!' That is the message I send by this letter. I want to be with you; my thoughts and affections are there. God bless you!

"If I were with you, I should speak of what a blessing are love, and kindred, and friendship, and hope, and memory, and all the bonds that bind us, a family, together; and I should recall, with gratitude, the name of him whom so many delight to honor.

"There are two characteristics which marked our ancestor, and that first generation of sons and daughters. I will call your attention to them as traits of character fit to be thought of now; and worthy of being repeatedly presented. I will name them, and then offer you a sentiment in connection with each.

"The first characteristic I refer to was, sympathy with the young, and love of childhood. They never frowned upon the innocent gayety of the young; they never felt that they themselves were too old, though it was indeed an old age that God led them to—too old to sympathize in the thoughts and pleasures of children. They never grew old in heart; there was a perennial fountain there. Many marked it; many of us, as we now recall our childhood, remember it with gratitude. They seemed to find peculiar happiness in contributing to the happiness of the young.

"I offer you then: 'Benjamin' and 'Joseph,' and the brethren of Joseph and Benjamin—men of our Israel; ever did they love 'the *children* of Israel.'

The second characteristic I would speak of was, quick sympathy and deep-seated philanthropy. Reference to a single incident shall tell all I have to say upon this, and lead to the sentiment I offer.

"You have all heard it related, that the cruel treatment of a slave, by the first settled minister of Walpole, so roused the righteous indignation of our ancestor, Colonel Bellows, that he said: 'I settled that man, and I will unsettle him;' and before many weeks the union between that minister and his people was dissolved.

"I offer you as a sentiment: 'The philanthropy of our ancestor, and his sympathy with the slave; may his descendants ever have an ear open to the cry of the oppressed. May they sustain the cause of God and humanity: Union with God, though it dissolve every other union.'

"My friends, those fathers have given to us those hills, covered with forests, where every morning now the mists, which go up from the river, rest a while, as if to look back upon the beauty of the valley below, before they go up higher. Those fathers have given us the valley also, the place of homes. This word, then, I will add: 'The monuments which we would rear to the memory of our fathers: may the God who gives the green in the spring-time, and in the autumn the brown and the scarlet, touch with His finger the work of our hands.'

"In bonds of love and kindred, I am your affectionate friend,

"FREDERICK N. KNAPP."

After reading this letter, Rev. H. W. Bellows said:

He could not sit down without asking his kinsmen to join him in an expression of affectionate sympathy with their absent cousin, whom severe lameness confined to his chair at home. This was no small trial to Mr. Knapp, who ought really to be considered as the prime instigator as well as constant furtherer of the present delightful gathering; whose whole heart and soul had been in the preparations, and who was here now in every thing but the body—a very important exception, unhappily, for them and the occasion. If he were not wholly mistaken, the conception of a monument to our Founder originated with "Cousin Fred," (he did not like to call his whole name, because it wasn't Bellows;) at any rate, he furnished the plans, selected the artist, Mr. Billings, who drew the emblems and designed the monument, engaged the marble-workers, who carried out the plan, and secured the assistance of the classic and accomplished gentleman, Professor Folsom, who put into idiomatic and conventional form the inscriptions. He confessed to a little reluctance in announcing the fact, that they had suffered themselves to go out of the family for the requisite learning, taste, or judgment involved in any part of the undertaking. But here, perhaps, was the place to say, that the science of inscriptions was a specialty, and that an accomplished poet or elegant writer might commit as great blunders as the merest tyro in the style of such a composition. Every one must observe, in the present instance, that a certain stiffness, formality, and absence of musical flow mark the inscriptions. They are not natural, easy, and in accordance with the style of the best literature. And they are not meant to be. They are carved in marble, and aim to partake of its squareness and rigidity; they are intended for all time, and avoid whatever belongs exclusively to the present. The whole sense is with a difficult fidelity to the rules, compressed within a single sentence, that he who begins shall be compelled to finish it; while each line has a complete meaning, and all together tells just and only just what is necessary. To be short but full, condensed yet intelligible, stately but unassuming, expressive to the present age, and not obscure to future generations; this requires an art, which is very little likely to be appreciated by those who have not given a careful and special attention to the subject. Volumes have been written on this topic; but he did not intend to add another at that time. Suffice it to say, in acknowledging their great indebtedness to Mr. Folsom, who made two journeys to Brookline, and spent many hours in perfecting the classic and elegantly-learned inscriptions of the monument, which, he dare say, many supposed could have flowed from the pen of any ready writer; that he claimed for the Committee the credit of having exhibited the family taste and learning in a most favorable light, in showing that they were learned enough to appreciate their own ignorance, and wise enough and tasteful enough to know just where to go to supply their deficiencies.

But this was wandering a little from Mr. Knapp, except that they were indebted to Mr. Knapp for Professor Folsom's interest in the monument. He would only add, however, that the town and the family were accustomed to feelings of obligation to his cousin Frederick. For he loved Walpole with an intelligent, fore-looking, and practical affection; was always considering how it might be decorated or improved; was most largely concerned in the origination, as he was eloquently employed in the consecration, of the cemetery; a planter of trees in its streets, and of families, valuable to its social well-being or its industry, upon its hill-sides. While his reputation as a faithful and successful minister, at his Massachusetts home, was dear to the family, his attachment and fidelity to his New-Hampshire birth-place was equally honorable to him, and grateful to his fellow-citizens and kindred; and he called upon his cousins to unite in cheering his long confinement and present disappointment with a hearty expression of affectionate regret at his absence, and lively gratitude for his invaluable services.

The company responded with thorough unanimity and entire cordiality to these sentiments; and but for the lack of any thing stronger than water, not excepting tea and coffee, would have drunk Mr. Knapp's health in a more grateful manner.

After Mr. Bellows had spoken, Rev. J. N. Bellows spoke.

Rev. J. N. Bellows, of Wilton, New-Hampshire, said: He had been requested to respond to the sentiments contained in the letter of his friend and cousin, the Rev. F. N. Knapp, respecting the general principle of philanthropy and our particular duties to the young; and that he was glad on this occasion to have the opportunity of alluding to what seemed to him an important principle, namely, the recognition of the moral influence of descent: the influence of progenitors upon their descendants. One may well inquire who were his ancestors, and what they were, when he himself is so much the creature, by nature, of their tastes and habits. To know one's self, one must know his ancestors.

The recognition of this principle in descent is gathering, here and there, families, over our land, who feel the value of private family histories in the education of their offspring, and giving a value to family gatherings beyond the pleasure of a social occasion, and the satisfaction of curiosity. And then how obvious is the truth that children will be likely to be what their parents are. Precepts are valueless unless followed by example. Would we see our children growing up in the paths of religious principle, we must be religious ourselves.

The speaker dwelt at some length upon the influence of home; the importance of the family bond; upon family religion; he earnestly entreated his kindred to seek a practical religion; and he closed his remarks with an affectionate allusion to the absence of his cousin and brother in the Christian ministry.

After Mr. Bellows had finished his remarks, as the evening was somewhat advanced, Mr. J. N. Knapp rose and said:

Friends and relatives, as it is about time for me to retire, I will offer you a sentiment of congratulation and good wishes:

"The virtues of the Founder of Walpole: A rich family bank; may his descendants annually enlarge its capital, and no stockholder ever sell out."

The whole company spontaneously rose as Mr. Jacob Knapp, at this point, left the room.

The following toast was next offered:

"John Kilburn and his heroic wife, brave pioneers: they will be conspicuous in the history of Walpole."

This toast was followed by some remarks from Dr. Morse, upon the influence of the departed on the living.

As some reference had been made to woman's bravery, Mr. Edward B. Grant rose, and spoke as follows:

In the infancy of the republic, and in the stormy times preceding the Revolution, man, as ever, was cheered in every difficulty by the sympathy and aid of woman; worthy mothers of those patriots, who, at every personal sacrifice, determined to break the galling chain that bound them to England.

Woman, ever faithful, shared with our fathers the privations and hardships through which at last their liberty, and that of unborn generations, was secured.

What mean those noisy declaimers who talk of the feeble influence and crushed faculties of woman?

What school of learning, of moral endeavor, depends more on its teacher than the home upon its mother?

What influence of all the world's professors and teachers tells so strongly on the habit of a man's mind, as those gentle droppings from a mother's lips, which, day by day and hour by hour, grow into the enlarging stature of his soul, and live with it for ever?

They can hardly be mothers who aim at a broader and noisier field; they have forgotten to be daughters; they must needs have lost the hope of being wives.

Woman's true sphere is in the cheerful and happy homes, wherever they may be; whether in country or in town; in the crowded city, or in the log-cabin of those forerunners of civilization, the restless borderers, who, although shunning the haunts of man, yet gradually prepare the way for refinement and Christianity.

One of the greatest monarchs that ever sat upon a throne, (Napoleon, whose instinct discovered genius in whatever garb,) in a conversation with one of the many distinguished women with which his court was adorned, asked her in what way he could best promote the happiness of his subjects. The reply was: "*Educate the mothers of France.*"

Did not the answer indicate a true knowledge of human nature; for who can doubt that it is upon the early influences of home, that every community must rely for those principles of virtue and truth; of industry and humanity; of a love for the Infinite Father and his finite children, which are the only foundations of a good government, and of a happy people?

Yes, it is woman's province, within the holy circle of home, to instill into the minds of the children of the republic, its future rulers and law-givers, its artisans and merchants, its fathers and mothers of coming generations, the gentle truths of religion, of duty to God and man; to fit for the battle of life, to weave the light but invulnerable armor that shields from sin and temptation; to render *home* happy.

Home! that sweetest of words, that dearest of realities, the ever-sought refuge, both for the body and the mind, from the cares and perplexities of life. Home! this is woman's highest, noblest field of duty.

I will, therefore, offer as a sentiment:

"The memory of the mothers of that inflexible band of patriots, to whom we are indebted for whatever of influence and happiness we enjoy, as citizens of this great confederacy of States."

The following letters were now read:

Letter from Henry Adams Bellows, Esq., of Concord, N. H.:

"CONCORD, Oct. 10, 1854.

"GENTLEMEN: I had hoped until now to be present at the family gathering around the monument of our ancestor, Colonel Benjamin Bellows.

"But I regret to say, that my duties require my attendance at the court now in session at this place.

"Allow me to assure you, however, that I sympathize very heartily in this expression of affectionate veneration for the unblemished name and high character which he has bequeathed to his descendants.

"I will thank you to convey to such of our family as may be present to-morrow, assurances of my brotherly affection, and of regret for my absence on this occasion.

"I am, gentlemen, very cordially your kinsman,

"H. A. BELLOWS.

"BENJAMIN B. GRANT, and others, Committee.

"I propose the following sentiment:

"The descendants of Colonel Benjamin Bellows: May the virtues which adorned his life continue to reside among his descendants, and may they, although widely-scattered, be ever drawn together by the cords of affection, springing from a respect for the family character."

Letter from John S. Wells, Esq., of Exeter, N. H.:

"EXETER, N. H., Sept. 28, 1854.

"MY DEAR SIR: I deeply regret my inability to accept your kind invitation, to attend with my wife the family gathering of her kinsmen at the home of her ancestors, on the 11th of October next. But my engagements in the court, which will then be in session, are such, that they will deprive me of the pleasure of joining you.

"Aside from the object of the gathering, to lay the foundation of a monument, to commemorate the virtues of him who founded your beautiful town, and by his fearless bravery infused energy into every arm, and confidence into all hearts, in times of trial and personal danger, the meeting must be one of great social interest.

"The wild and terrific scenes of the French and Indian wars will, I presume, come up before you, both in song and story. The exciting occurrences of frontier life, as they will be recounted, will appear to the youth like tales of a vivid imagination; but when they realize the accuracy of the description of the murderous savage yells, and of the dying shrieks of the white men, who fell in defense of friends and home, it will thrill the life-blood of them all.

"The mind will be carried back to the early and rude condition of the territory, which the sagacious Founder selected to become the spot around which the hearts of his numerous descendants would cluster with deep and abiding affection, and with which the passing stranger is now so often delighted.

"Your hearts will all be pained when the misty figures of the departed kinsmen shall be brought up before you. Strong minds, and kind and noble hearts, lived in those airy forms. They were a happy and joyous people, they sat at generously-loaded boards, and the doors of their homes were always open. They regarded New-England as strong men cherish their fatherland, but loved their native Walpole with the intensity of woman's devotion.

"The splendid natural scenery around you will be referred to, as the great unchanged objects which link the present with the past; and it will, I fancy, delight you all to realize that so numerous a company of the descendants are placing their concentrated gaze upon those objects, which so often charmed and delighted their ancestors. Let them trace the winding Connecticut, threading its way through the rich and smooth-rolled meadows, to the far-off rolling sea. Then scan the wild and rugged hills and mountains, near and far away, tinged with the varied colors which the autumnal frosts of New-England peculiarly produce; and then say if, in all their wanderings, their eyes have rested upon scenery more beautiful than that which the Founder of Walpole was charmed to look upon.

"You will consider, in connection with the virtues of the man whose memory you design to perpetuate, the means adopted for that purpose; and I dare say will all agree that nothing more appropriate could be devised. I would that more columns were set up in our land, that the virtues of the good and great might be constantly kept in mind by the pillars erected to perpetuate the memory of their valued deeds. And may the monument which the descendants of Colonel Bellows design to erect, stimulate them and their descendants to that exertion which will insure them, if not the honor of bronze or marble columns, the love, gratitude, and respect, not only of kith and kin, but of all who love our country, and its cherished institutions. May they realize the value of a free government, and the cost and trials requisite to create and preserve it. May they regard our national Constitution as of priceless value, and resolve never to dim the lustre of the good name of their worthy ancestor, by sympathy with those who would prostrate that unmatched structure, which our revolutionary fathers set up, *the American Union.*

"Most respectfully yours,

"John S. Wells."

Letter from Abel Herbert Bellows, Esq., of Concord, N. H.:

"Concord, N. H., Tuesday evening, 10 P.M., Oct. 10, 1854.

"B. B. Grant, Esq., Chairman of the Monument Committee:

"Dear Sir: I regret extremely that professional engagements will prevent my being present at the consecration of the monument to the memory of our common ancestor; and that I can not join the family circle assembled to pay a tribute of respect to the name and virtues of one who was truly "*without fear and without reproach.*"

"It has occurred to me that while the material results of our ancestor's labors are palpable in the prosperous and thriving community which has sprung up around his first settlement, we may not perhaps have properly estimated the silent influence of his noble traits of character upon generation after generation of his descendants; for who can tell how often the light of that example, shining down upon us through a hundred years, may have prompted to the generous and disinterested act; or how often it may have revealed in their true colors, temptations to abandon the path of honor and rectitude? *This* is the great legacy he has bequeathed to us, more valuable than farms or meadow-lands, and for this does he deserve our gratitude, and the erection of a lofty monument; and I will therefore give you as a sentiment:

"Honesty and uprightness of character, illustrated in the life of Colonel Benjamin Bellows, pearls without price: May each of his descendants inherit them as *heirlooms*, and prize them as their choicest possession.

"I am, in great haste, very truly your friend and cousin,

"A. HERBERT BELLOWS."

Letter from Rev. Thomas Hill, of Waltham, Mass.:

"CONCORD, N. H., Oct. 9, 1854.

"B. B. GRANT, Esq.:

"MY DEAR SIR: I am sorry that professional duties will prevent my being with you on the 11th instant, and joining with you in the exercises of the day. Be assured that I am with you in the feeling of veneration for your honored ancestor, and that I am proud that my children also may claim a descent from him, whose noblest monument may be found in the records of the history of his State, and in the present and increasing prosperity of the town which he founded.

"Give my cordial good wishes to the members of the family that may assemble with you on Wednesday, and allow me to offer a Scriptural wish for the occasion:

"Walpole: 'It shall be said, This and that man was born in her; and the Highest himself shall establish her.'

"Yours very truly,

"THOMAS HILL."

The reading of the letters was followed by remarks from Rev. H. W. Bellows.

Rev. Mr. Bellows, in proposing the health of his absent cousins, H. A. Bellows, Esq., A. Herbert Bellows, Esq., Hon. Mr. Wells, Rev. Thomas Hill, G. G. Bellows, Esq., Mr. F. W. G. Bellows, and Mr. George Grant, all of whom had been confidently expected, and on whose presence the interest of the occasion so much depended, had a debt of obligation to acknowledge to Mr. Herbert Bellows in especial, for his patient and sagacious investigations at the State-House at Concord, which had supplied him with the most valuable materials for his address. He owed much also to Rev. Mr. Knapp, much to Mr. Lyman Watkins, much to Mr. Charles Lincoln, and much to his venerable aunts and uncles, Mrs. Robeson and Mr. Abel Bellows, for their contributions of facts, dates, and recollections. Mr. Lincoln, in particular, had kindly thrown open to him all the various sources, in which he had found any information touching the history of the town, which it was to be hoped he would finally carry out his purpose of writing in full; and Mr. Watkins, by his wonderful memory and curious taste for local anti quity, had revived or imparted valuable recollections. Dr. Morse, too, by his published sketches in the *Cheshire Gazette*, on which he had so freely drawn to-day, deserved his marked and grateful acknowledgments, which he was interested in making acceptable to him, as a propitiation for having stolen considerable of whatever animation belonged to the account of the Kilburn fight, from his writings. But far beyond any thanks due to these kindly helpers, went his gratitude to "Cousin Herbert," who had fairly exhausted the materials in the Capitol, and for weeks kept the mail freighted with his contributions of new facts and incidents bearing on the family history. Without his aid, the author of the address would not have been able to move a step. But besides general historical information, Mr. Herbert Bellows had contributed some of the best characterization, many of the most amusing anecdotes, and some of the happiest narrative in the address. True, it had all been worked over, but the author found it difficult to improve many of the thoughts and expressions in his cousin's off-hand sketches. He should be most ungrateful, not to make his kinsmen aware, that though deprived of Cousin Herbert's presence to-day, no one had contributed more substantially to the interest of the occasion, or had at heart a livelier sympathy with the ceremonies of the day.

In regard to the much-regretted absence of so many distinguished cousins, there was a ground of proud consolation. They were too important, and actively useful in their several posts of duty at home, to be assembled at any one place, on any given occasion, however interesting. The business of the country could not be stopped; the courts locked in their sessions; the ecclesiastical conventions robbed of their eloquence; judges, juries, and witnesses brought to a stand; pulpits, parishes, and patients vacated and abandoned, that their family meeting might go on more successfully, and with the decoration of all its jewels! No! the pillars of society must stand in their places, and not gather about the monument of our Founder; and considering that their absent cousins were performing Atlantean duty, and keeping the cope of the social system from falling in, he thought a proud satisfaction might be wrung from the bitter disappointment their absence had caused, in a generous construction of the social necessity for it. He proposed the health of "The professional members of the family absent on this occasion," with this sentiment, excusing their absence from our ranks on this monumental occasion:

"The pillars of society can not move in family columns."

Rev. Dr. Bellows desired, as a final word, to convey to the President of the occasion, B. F. Grant, Esq., his own, and he was sure the universal, thanks of the company, for his invaluable services in every part of the long and laborious enterprise, so happily crowned to-day. When it was recollected that some 1200 descendants of Colonel Bellows had to be hunted up; their names, history, and present abode discovered and considered; that guesses and estimates of their willingness and ability to aid the monumental effort, had to be shrewdly made, that every body's feelings might be duly regarded; that circulars must be skillfully written, printed, and distributed, twice or thrice over; that a varied and curious correspondence, involving much labor, was to be managed discreetly; that pecuniary responsibility must be assumed in advance of collections; that the grounds of the monument must be chosen and arranged, and its foundations laid; its fence selected, ordered, obtained, and erected; the bulky monument brought here from Boston, and all the necessary apparatus for its elevation procured; that the time for this meeting, the invitations, and the arrangement for it, had all, at no small cost of calculation, providence, and taste, to be harmoniously, efficiently, and punctually contrived and carried into execution; when we considered all this, and then remembered that Mr. Grant had been the Chairman of the Committee, the Secretary, correspondent, travelling agent, (for one journey to Boston he knew him to have made in this business,) fence-builder, head-mason, land-surveyor, and universal stirrer-up of matters; above all, the financier and caterer, and now finally the presiding officer at the consecration and the festival; he felt that the company would join him in congratulating their President on the universal success of his efforts; and unite in a vote of heartfelt thanks for the time and skill, the good-will and patient continuance, the business-like regularity and gentlemanly feeling, above all, the genuine family spirit he had exhibited throughout the whole affair; and now, more especially, for his kind offices in presiding over the feast, which, with the cordial and skillful aid of their gentle cousins, he had provided for the occasion.

The company heartily responded to these sentiments.

After Mr. Bellows had spoken, all joined in singing the last ode, to the tune of *Auld Lang Syne.*

ADDENDA.

WILL AND AUTOGRAPH OF JOHN, THE FIRST BELLOWS IN AMERICA.

At the last moment, while the press is waiting, I have been able, through the kindness of Frederic Kidder, Esq., a distinguished antiquarian, to obtain from the records of Middlesex, Mass., a copy of several papers, making it clear and without a shadow of doubt, that John Bellows, who came over in the "Hopewell," in 1635, was the identical John, who, on the 9th May, 1655, married Mary Wood, at Concord. By a deposition he made 15th January, 1669, John Bellows, of Marlborough, was then about forty-four years of age, which corresponds as accurately as could be expected from statements necessarily inexact, with the computed age of the John Bellows, who, in 1635, was twelve years old.

Taking this fact, then, as established, it is most interesting to see that this unknown boy, of twelve, landing in the wilderness, had succeeded in making a substantial place for himself in the new world, as a farmer of the better sort. And this fact is evidenced by the precious document below, being the last will of John Bellows, of Marlboro', with the inventory of his property annexed, from which an exact idea can be formed of his station in life, and of the general condition of the better sort of farmers at the early date of 1683, when he died. If we consider the newness of the country, and the great value of money at that time, his estate will appear quite substantial, while his household goods will indicate what was then decided comfort—however unsatisfactory it might be now. It is gratifying to be able to trace our Founder back to a young pilgrim of twelve, who possessed the boyish energy to emigrate to the New World, and to make his way to such respectability and comfort as the last will and testament of John Bellows, of Marlboro', indicates. I judge from the inventory, that John Bellows was either brought up a carpenter at home, or acquired and practised that trade in connection with his farming in New-England. Tradition had made him out a physician; but his will, I think, proves him a carpenter—a calling nobody need be ashamed to associate with his own or an ancestor's name. The signature to the will is a copy of a tracing from his autograph appended to a deposition he made in 1668. The signature to his will is written in so weak a hand, as not to be significant of his character.

I am compelled to believe that the reason of Benjamin, our Founder's father, not being mentioned in his father's will, is because from his birth he had been adopted into the Moore family, by whom, according to a tradition, he was brought up. There is another hypothesis, that he was born after his father's death. Daniel, I suppose, died without issue.

To show to what large possessions the grandson of John, namely, our Founder, had attained, I add a copy of his will, which may be advantageously compared with the older document:

WILL OF JOHN BELLOWS, SEN., OF MARLBOROUGH.

I, John Bellows, Senr., of Marlborough, in New-England, being weak in body but of sound understanding, do make & ordain my last Will and Testament in manner & forme following, viz.: *Imprs.* After my debts are paid, I give and bequeath unto Mary, my loving wife, unto her own use & dispose, & to remain in her hands for as long as she pleaseth, as her own proper goods, one Cow wch came of a cow yt I had of Mrs. Mary Rowlandson; also an Heifer which came of the sd Cow which is now two years old. Also One Calfe of this present year, likewise my bigest brass kettle & my lesser Iron pott & the bigger of my Two brass skelletts. *Item.* I will yt my lands in Marlborough aforesaid & myne other moveable goods shall be disposed of unto my Children namely Isaac, John, Thomas, Eleazar, Nathaniel, Mary and Abigail, When they shall be of ye age of one & Twenty years or married; My son Isaac shall have a double portion of my estate wch remains beside wt I have given unto his mother (as above sd) and each of the rest of my said Children shall have half as much portion as my son Isaac hath.

Item. I have already bequeathed unto my daughter Abigail Lawrence, as so much of her portion, One Two years old heifer, and one Cow calf of this present year, and a sow of Two years old, and one Iron pot & the worth of Ten shillings in other small things. Furthermore I leave Mary my loving wife whole Executrix of this my Will and Testamt., & she shall have her maintenance from my estate, for so long as she shall remain my widdow.

Finally I desire, & appoint my loving friends Joseph Rice and Joseph Newton to be the Overseers of this my last Will & Testament. In witness whereof I the said John Bellows, senr. do hereunto put my hand & seale, this nineteenth day of June, One thousand, Six hundred, eighty & three.

In presence of
John Woods
Isaac Amsden.

Octob: 2. 83 Sworn in Court by the sd witnesses as attests. Tho. Danforth R.
Middlesex Prob. Recds.
Lib. VI. fol. 93.

An Inventory of the Goods & Chattells of John Bellows deceased, late of Marlborough in New-England, taken by Deacon Solomon Johnson, Abraham How, John Wood partly on the 6th prtly on the 8th August, 1683.

		lb.
Imprs.	Two Oxen	008.
	Five Cows	12
	Three 2 years old	6
	Five Calves of this yeare	2.10
	One Mare 3lb. Two yearlings 2lb.	5.
	One Cart & Wheels	1.
	Hoop and Boxes	0.12.
	Cops & pin & yoake	04.
	One Timber Chain & one whipple-tree chain	10.
	A pair of fetters	04.
	A broad ax, & four narrow ones	14.
	One Iron Bar & one Share-mould	08.06.
	One Cross cut Saw	08.
	Two Hand-saws & one Tenon-saw	04.
	Two hollow Adses	06.
	One draught-Share & two round Shares	05.
	One Square & Three Augurs	05.
	Three & Twenty Plane-irons bigger & lesser	11.06
It.	Four Gouges	00.03
	Four broad Chissels. 3s. & seven Heading Chissels. 4s. 6d.	07.06
	One Wimble & two Bits & a small saw	02.06
	Two Froes. 3s. 6d. & one Spade 5s.	08.06
	One pr of Stirrup-irons, Two old files & a Chissell	02.
	Two Turning Irons & a pr of old Compasses	02.

Three Harrow Hoes 6s. one old broad ax, and one old Ads	09.
One Beetle and Three Wedges	05.
Two old Hoes, & one old Ax & many small pieces of old iron	03.
Two Broad Hoes 5s., & one plough & share, & Bolt 6s.	11.
One Cart-rope and Two Forks	04.
Two Trammels, one pair of Tongs, and an old fire-pan	08.
One Back-sword, & Two Barrels of guns, ye sword 12s. the Barrels 8s., and One Hammer 1s.	01.01.00
Two Iron Potts, and Two pair of pot-hooks . .	01.
Two old brass Kettles, and Two brass Skellets . .	01.
Nine yds Searge 2s. p yd. 3 yds Kersy 3s p yd . .	1.07
One old Warming-pan, and an old Frying pan . .	03.
Three small Pewter-platters, one salt-seller & 6 Spoons	08.
Treys & Wooden Dishes 8s. Glass bottles & earthenware 2s. 6d. One old brazen Pot-lid 6d.	11.
Five Swine, & Three little pigs, & Two sucking pigs	03.
Two bed-tikings and one Bolster	01.
Two Bed-blankets, and Two feather-pillows . .	01.03.06
Thirty pounds of Hemp from ye brake 10s. Flax from ye brake	1.02.
One flock-bed & two pillows 10s. One rug & 2 Cover lids	02.16.
Seven sheets 2lb. 4s. four pillow-drawers, & a table cloth, four shillings	02.08.
One remnant of new linnen 2s. & some remnants of old, 4s.	06.
4 Barrels 6s. a Churn & 2 Tubb 6s. 4 Pails 3s. 6d. .	00.15.06
One little Table, and Three Chairs 6s. Two sivs 2s. .	08.
One woollen Wheel, and one Linnen Wheel	05.
Books 7s. One Chest. One meal-trough, One Box 10s. .	17.
His wearing Clothes	01.10.
Four Bushels of Indian, and four of Ry	01.04.
Wheat, Rie & Pease of this years growth, one grindstone a shilling	01.05
Indian Corn now on ye ground	04.10
Flax of this year, & a pair of Cards 11s. & Provisions 1lb.	01.11
The Home-lot with all ye out-lands, both Up-lands & Meadows, & Cedar-swamp p taining to the home-lot, together with the dwelling-hous & Orchard thereon	60
Debts due to this Estate from several p sons . . .	05.
Ye sum total	135.11.06
	1.07.00
	136.18.06

Oct 2. 83. Sworn by Mary Bellows
Execr in Court.

COPY OF THE LAST WILL OF COLONEL BENJAMIN BELLOWS.

In the name of God, Amen:

I, Benjamin Bellows, of Walpole, in the County of Cheshire and State of New-Hampshire, Esq., being of health of body, and of perfect mind and memory, thanks be given to God therefor, and calling to mind the mortality of my body, and knowing that it is appointed for all men once to die, do make and ordain this my last will and testament; that is to say, principally and first of all, I do give and recommend my soul into the hands of Almighty God that gave it; and my body I recommend to the earth, to be buried in a decent Christian manner, at the discretion of my executor, nothing doubting, but at the general resurrection I shall receive the same again by the mighty power of God; and as touching such wordly estate wherewith it has pleased God to bless me with in this life, I give and devise and dispose of the same in the following manner and form: and, first of all, I give and bequeath to my beloved wife, Mary Bellows, the improvement of the one third part of my now dwelling-house, and the third part of my now improved lands in Walpole, with the improvement of my barn on the east side of the road, so long as she, the said Mary, shall continue my widow. I also give to my said wife one yoke of oxen, three cows, and one horse, which she shall please to choose out of my stock; also a cart, plough, yoke, and chain, all which she is to have the improvement of during her life, then, *then* to be returned, or the like stock, to my children; and I further give to my said wife one third part of all my household furniture, to be set off to her to dispose of as she shall think fit amongst my children as she shall see cause. I also give her a side-saddle and bridle, and fifty pounds lawful money, to be paid her when she shall call for the same; and if my said wife shall see cause to marry, then the improvement of my house and lands to return to my children, that is, willed to her, she has done with them, and in lieu thereof, to have a hundred dollars per year, paid her by my children, to be equally divided, that is, about eleven dollars each per year.

Imprimis. I give to my well-beloved son, Peter Bellows, and his children, two whole rights of land in Rockingham, in the County of Cumberland and State of New-York, containing about seven hundred acres, and is No. two and No. three in the twentieth range of lots in said town, and lies altogether as by the plan may appear, and is the rights drawn to the names of Benjamin French and Peter Bellows. I also give to him and his children six hundred acres of land in Walpole, and *lyeth* above the Great Falls on Connecticut River; said land *lyeth* in Walpole, and bounds west on said river;

north on land called the Governor's farm; east on my own land, and south on land of Col. Atkinson. Also the ninth parts of all the lands I shall leave in Rockingham undisposed of, which, together with the lands I have given him by deed in Charlestown, to be the full part and portion out of my estate, with one yoke of oxen, two cows, and a horse, and one hundred pounds in cash, to be laid out to finish his house, and fifty pounds to *cloath* his family.

Impr. I give and bequeath to my well-beloved son, Benjamin Bellows, four hundred acres of land in Walpole; bounded south on the town line; west on land sold to one Burt and one Fisk; north on land sold to William Smeed; east on land of *Botbut*, Nicholas, and Maj'r Richardson, and the ninth part of what land I shall leave undisposed of in Rockingham, which, together with what I have given him by deed, and the fourth part of all my estate which may be left, not disposed of after my estate is settled and paid out all legacies; also I give him one hundred pounds for his trouble in settling my estate; and I further give him one yoke of oxen, two cows, and a horse.

Impr. I give to my well-beloved son, John Bellows, a certain piece of land in Walpole aforesaid, and contains about four hundred acres, be the same more or less; and it begins at the north-east corner of a hundred acre lot given him by deed, and to run north ten degrees; east till it comes to the south line of Col. Atkinson's land; then runs west on Col. Atkinson's land till it comes to what he has a deed of, till it comes to Connecticut River; and I further give him four hundred acres of land east of the line given heretofore, to *lye* in a square form, where he shall pitch the same, and this, with the ninth part of what land I shall leave unsold in Rockingham, with what I have heretofore given him deed of, to be his full part and share in my estate, except one yoke of oxen, two cows, and a horse, which is to be given out of my stock.

Impr. I give to my well-beloved son, Joseph Bellows, all my lands which I have in *Leu*ningburgh, that he has not heretofore a deed of; as also what land I have in a town in New-Hampshire, called Mason, being half of a right drawn to the name of John Butterfield; also all the land I have in the township of Rindge, which was about five hundred acres, but part of it is sold to pay taxes; also two hundred acres in the township of Fitzwilliam, as may appear drawn to me, and I further give him the ninth part of what land I shall leave undisposed of in the township of Rockingham, which, together with what he has a deed of, to be his part of my estate, except one yoke of oxen, two cows, and a horse, which I further give him out of my stock.

Impr. I give to my well-beloved daughter, Abigail Bellows, my house and land I bought of Moses Brown, on the east side of the road to Westmoreland; as also fifty acres of the lot Denison lives on, on the south side, and about twenty-three acres adjoining, called "Mepas" lot, which land I give to her and heirs of her body for ever, not to be disposed of out of the family. Said lands contain about one hundred and thirty acres, the house, and the house Doctor Ashley lives in. I do also give to my said daughter Abigail the one third part of all my household furniture after my decease, to be kept for her till she comes to the age of twenty-one or *marry's;* the improvement of said lands be for her use improved by my executor, till she comes to age; and I further give her the sixth part of all my personal estate that shall be left after my estate is settled; and I give her the ninth part of all my lands that I shall not dispose of in Rockingham; and I further give my daughter forty acres of land, being the land Daniel Bixby lives on, which I give to her and her heirs for ever, bounded north on land of Aaron Hodskins; west on land of Delano; south on lands of *hinds*; east on Bundy. I also give her one yoke of oxen, two cows, and a horse, and one hundred pounds in money, which is her portion of my estate.

Impr. I give to well-beloved son, Theodore Bellows, about eighty acres of meadow land and about two hundred acres of upland, lying adjoining to the land given to John Bellows, and south of his land, beginning at an oak stump in the corner of John Bellows's land fence, and runs north, as the fence runs to the river, about twenty-six rods; then runs down by the river about one hundred and fifty rods to a walnut tree, marked near the end of the ditch; then runs on the ditch; goes through the meadow to the end of the ditch; then to run east by the needle about four hundred rods to the line of John Bellows's land to a white oak tree, marked for a corner; then to run north on John Bellows's land, as the same is marked to a corner, being a white oak; then to run west on his land to the first-mentioned stump. And I also give about two hundred and forty acres to my said son Theodore, called my great pasture, bounded west on land of Col. Atkinson; south on land of Jona'n Hall; east partly on land of Babcock and the road as it is now fenced; and north on land of John Bellows; and I further give my son Theodore three hundred pounds in money, to be paid him by my executors, to help build him a house and barn, to be laid out for that use by my executors; as also the ninth part of what lands I shall leave undisposed of in Rockingham, and the fourth part of what estate shall be left, both real and personal, in Walpole, and part of my live stock, namely, one yoke of oxen, two cows, and one horse, also a cart, yoke, and chain.

Impr. I give to my beloved son, Thomas Bellows, about three hundred and fifty acres of land and meadow in Walpole aforesaid, with all the buildings thereon, being the house and land I now live on and improve, reserving to his mother the part I heretofore willed her. Said land begins at the walnut tree marked, at the river at the end of the ditch being the south-west corner of Theodore's land, and runs down the river one hundred and twenty rods to a walnut stump, with a stake and some stones about it near the lower fence; then runs east through the meadow till it comes to the meadow fence; then runs south about twenty rods as the fence stands to a corner; then runs east to a great white pine, so as to take the spring, and so to continue east by the needle till it comes to the line of John Bellows's land; then runs northerly on said John's land, as the same is marked on trees, to the south-east corner of Theodore's land; then runs west by Theodore's land to the east end of the ditch, so on the ditch to the first-mentioned corner. And I further give to my said son Thomas three hundred acres of land on the east line of said town, to begin at Col. Atkinson's corner, and run south to the end of the *lotts* laid out, being about two hundred and sixty rods; then to run west as the lot *lyeth* and on Col. Atkinson's till it makes three hundred acres; and I give him the ninth part of what land I leave unsold in Rockingham, and the fourth part of the estate I shall leave undisposed of in Walpole, and I give him one yoke of oxen, two cows, and a horse, also a cart, yoke, and chain.

Impr. I give to my well-beloved daughter, Molley Bellows, about two hundred and fifty acres of land and meadow in Westminster, in the County of Cumberland and New State, so called, adjoining to Connecticut River, being the nine first meadow *lotts* in the Governour's meadow, so called, and four fifty acre lots, being No. twenty-two, twenty-three in the first range of fifty acre lots, and No. twenty-six in the second range of fifty acres, and another fifty acre lot I had of Bildad Andrews, with all the buildings thereon, which I give to my said daughter Molley and the heirs of her body forever, not to be disposed of from them. I also give to my said daughter the one third part of all my household furniture, which I shall leave to be set off to her, and kept safe by my executors for her till she comes to the age of twenty-one or *Marrye's*, and the improvement of said lands to be for her use to bring her up at the discretion of my executors, and I further give her the ninth part of all my land that I shall not dispose of in Rockingham, and one yoke of oxen, two cows, and a horse, and one hundred pounds in money, which is her part of my estate.

Impr. I give to my well-beloved son, Josiah Bellows, about four hundred acres of land and meadow in Walpole, and beginning at a walnut stump and stake and stones, being the south-west corner of Thomas Bellows's land, and runs south on the river till it comes to land of Doctr. Chase; then east on said Chase's land and runeth to the meeting house land; thence on that and land of Mr. Sparhawk and Mr. Fessenden to the north end of his land; then runs east by said Fessenden's land to land Trotts; then on land of John Kilburn; then on land till it comes to Moses Stearns; then on land of Stearns about north-west to a road; then on said road till it comes to Thomas Bellows; then west on his land to the first mentioned corner by the river. Also a *lott* of land, called Jonathan Jennison's *lott*, being about one hundred acres, and bounded *soth* on land of Mr. Sparhawk, west on Kilbourn's, and north on Hartwell, east on Bordman. And I give him about thirty-three acres of land in Westminster, being a house lot and three meadow *lotts* where my potash house is. And I also give him the ninth part of what land I shall leave in Rockingham, and three hundred pounds in money, to help build him a house and barn; and I further give him the fourth part of all my lands which is not here willed, and the fourth part of my personal estate not disposed of, and one yoke of oxen, two cows, and a horse, and a cart yoke and chain.

Impr. I give to the town of Walpole one hundred acres of land in Walpole for the use of a *Gramer Scholl* to be kept at the *Scholl* house near where the meeting house now stands, provided the town will clear and put under improvement sixty acres of the land in six years, which improvement is to be *lett* for the use of said *Scholl* and no other use made thereof; said land to be laid out by a committee, where it is not heretofore disposed of.

Impr. I give to my daughter in law, Mary Willard, a seventy acre lot in Keene, on the east line of the town, according as the same is laid out; and I give it to her and her children born of her.

Impr. I give to my son in law, John Jennison, fifty acres of land in Walpole, north of the road to Alstead, in a good form, to be laid where he shall pitch the same between the road and Col. Atkinson's land, not before disposed of, for one of his sons.

Impr. I give to my son in law, Jonathan Jennison, a cow and heifer two years old, and what money he owes to me, to be discharged by my executors.

And my will further is, that all my lands and personal estate, if any be found after that my debts and charges be paid, be equally divided among my nine children, and the will further is, if it should please God to take any of my children out of the world before they have children of their own, then the estate I give them be equally divided between the rest of my surviving children. And I do hereby appoint my well-beloved wife, Mary Bellows, and my son, Benjamin Bellows, to be my executors to this my last will and testament. And I hereby give my executors full power to give deed to any and all persons that I have contracted with for lands; they fulfilling their contracts *precisely* and paying the same fully up, according to their bargains. And I do hereby utterly disallow and revoke and disannul all and every other former wills and testaments by me heretofore made, in any way before. Ratifying and confirming this to be my last will and testament.

In witness whereof I have hereunto set my hand and seal this twenty-third day of June, Anno Domini 1777.

Signed, pronounced and declared this my last will and testament in presence of Elisha Harding.

Martin Ashley, B. Bellows. [Seal.]

Joseph Douglas.

The foregoing will was proved in the usual form by

Thos Sparhawk, J. Probate.

Recorded by Ichabod Fisher, Redgr. Probate.

OUR RECENT GRAVES.

Among the most interesting recollections connected with our family-life within the last generation, are those of the losses we have sustained by death. Few family circles have in one generation more of worth, promise, and beauty to deplore than our own. Who of us can forget the scientific attainments, the natural qualifications for his profession, the charming personal attributes, the early fame, and the large promise that were prematurely buried in the grave of Dr. George Bellows?* Had he lived, he would have been one of the most distinguished ornaments of the medical profession, as he was already the idol of his neighborhood, and the pride of his family. His death, ministered to by the love of friends who hurried from Walpole to his bedside, cast a gloom over a wide circle of kindred, with whom his memory is still green, though nearly thirty winters have beaten on his grave. The sweet voices of his sisters, Eliza and Fanny Anne, the last of whom died in early womanhood, are also hushed, but continue to sing on in the ears that loved their heart-music.

Nor was cousin George the only "beloved physician" the grave has claimed from our family. We are still grieving over the loss of our distinguished kinsman, Dr. Abel Bellows Robeson, whose remains were so recently laid in the family tomb at Walpole. "The only son of his mother, and she a widow," Dr. Robeson, the playmate of the writer's youth, was sent at an early age to Yale College, where he graduated in 1835. Here he formed the intimacy, which ended in marriage, with the daughter of the distinguished theologian and professor, Dr. Taylor, of New-Haven, a union which was the blessing of his life. After a very careful and enthusiastic study of his profession in the best medical schools of the country, Dr. Robeson established himself in New-York as a physician. His rare zeal and aptness for his calling, soon recommended him to the appointing powers, as a hospital physician; and he passed years of most laborious duty in the thankless but instructive walks of the asylums of the poor, the fever-worn emigrant, the wounded laborer, the sick and wasting foreigner. Such are the emulation and competition in the medical practice of New-York, that it requires an immense patience and overwhelming merits to secure a lucrative foothold there. Yet the splendor of the prize held out to success is so great that hundreds, who ultimately fail, are tempted to enter the lists. Dr. Robeson struggled earnestly with all the usual difficulties, and with the added ones of a naturally feeble constitution, and a pride of character that permitted no stooping to conquer. Early married, and with a

---

* Son of Joseph, and brother of H. A. Bellows, Esq.

rapidly-growing family, without fortune or influential friends, subject to sudden and lingering attacks of illness, he yet advanced, and, keeping all the ground he made, finally reached the threshold from which the path to success was sure and easy; and, at this moment, with all the doubtful, the soul-wasting and body-destroying labor done, and all the pleasant rewards unreaped, he died, in the prime of life and the midst of usefulness, and in open view of a most flattering and lucrative professional success.

Dr. Robeson's medical sagacity was of a rare order. He had the professional confidence of the very heads of his own calling. Patient and untiring in the study and observation of his cases, he often saved lives despaired of by other physicians. As a nurse he was unrivalled; tender, ingenious, sympathetic, and cautious, he could contrive medicines, suggest food, and invent comfortable appliances to meet every temper, age, and complaint. And the suffering his skill could not cure, his engaging company solaced, and his warm affections alleviated. Full of humor, a store-house of anecdote, a kind and quick appreciator of other's gifts, intuitively acquainted with men, possessing a large and varied knowledge of the world, he was, among his established patients or familiar friends, one of the most agreeable companions in the world. Too proud for his own peace, asking no favors, and spurning mean actions, sensitive to blame, and irritable by constitution and invalidism, he had great obstacles to popular success in a certain haughtiness and reserve of manner, which yielded only to overtures and advances from others. But nothing could exceed the goodness and generosity of his heart, the loyalty of his friendships, the breadth of his sympathies. His great professional struggles, his constant ill-health, his pride and his infirmities, often concealed his affections or perverted the apparent course of them. But he loved his kindred, in their remotest branches, with a singular warmth, and passed many of his hours in New-York in talking over, one by one, the friends he so rarely visited at Walpole.

Dr. Robeson had finally secured a practice of the best sort, and in the most flattering circle, in the city of New-York, when he died. His memory is very dear to all his old patients. They saw his courage, his uncomplaining fortitude, his elastic spirits, his victory over repeated violent sicknesses in his own person, as well as over their own complaints; and they honored the brave man as well as the sagacious and kind physician. This tribute is due to his memory from one who had his gay companionship in childhood, his tender professional care in middle life, his confidence and affections always; who lived in the same city, and saw and shared his struggles for an honorable name; who can testify to the fortitude and submission with which he met the last messenger, and to the large charity with all men, and the humble dependence on God's mercy in which he died. This record is made here, that his children may know the esteem in which their father was held in the city where they were born.

Catherine, daughter of Josiah Bellows, 1st, and wife of H. A. Bellows, Esq., of Concord, N. H., was one of the most exalted and intelligent women our family has produced. She united strength of intellect with gentleness of heart, a large interest in universal themes with a punctilious fidelity to domestic duties. Formed for meditation and study, an admirable talker and most sympathetic listener, she yet discharged the duties of the wife and the mother with a true New-England loyalty of heart and hand. Duty was her watchword. Dwelling through her married life, far from her kindred, and on the northern frontiers of the State, where domestic cares are multiplied and embarrassed by many obvious causes; delicate in constitution, and fitted rather for ease and dependence than for grave and constant responsibility, she never flinched from her post, and earned the repute of a faithful, competent, hospitable, and brave-hearted woman. The beauty of her brow, the heavenly purity and softness of her blue eye, never exceeded by any within the writer's observation, spoke the fine proportions and transparent purity and celestial aspirations of the soul tabernacled within. Full of faith and resignation, this gentle and thoughtful woman, large-minded and high-hearted, passed away, leaving her husband and children, and the circle of her kindred, permanent mourners over so much perished worth and power.

Sufficient reference has been made in the report of the family meeting to the loss the family met in the death of Edward Stearns Bellows, son of John, son of Joseph. Yet, to perpetuate his memory, we transfer to this more enduring record the obituary notice which appeared in the *Boston Courier* of May 26, 1837:

"Died, near Adrian, Michigan, about the 30th of March last, Edward S. Bellows, Esq., son of John Bellows, Esq., of Walpole, N. H.

"Mr. Bellows, in the pursuit of his professional duties, which he had just entered upon at Adrian, was obliged to go some distance into the thinly-settled country, north of his residence. Having reached a point beyond which there was no stage conveyance, he attempted to reach his destination on foot, through a forest, and alone; for no guide could be procured. After eleven days, his friends became alarmed at his absence, and went in search of him. He was found dead in the woods, with no marks of violence upon his person; and there are sufficient grounds for believing that, having lost his way, and, after some search, discovering it, he had seated himself to rest before pursuing his journey; and, overcome with fatigue, want of food, and cold, he had given way to sleep, and was soon chilled to death.

"It is perhaps well the public should know something of the remarkable young man it has lost. No one ever so much as saw him, without being struck with the dignity and power of his apparent character. Nobility, generosity, and elevation of mind shone in his face and mien. His pride might repulse many. He was one of whom most would form a less favorable opinion than he deserved; for his reserve, haughtiness of demeanor, his impatience of control, independence of thought, and self-reliance, are qualities which, however necessarily connected with the higher order of minds, in certain stages of their progress, are yet never understood or tolerated by the crowd.

"Perhaps no young man, having his friends among those capable of judging, ever left behind him a more enthusiastic admiration of his talents. Few can know the difficulties he surmounted, His intellectual ardor subdued all circumstances. His own yearnings for truth had been the only guide of his studies until the last three years of his life. The intense pursuit of his profession had not interfered with a wide range of other studies; for, although persuaded that the law is a science to be mastered only with a life, he was not willing that life should be devoted to it. He aimed to know enough of it to be faithful and successful in its practice. He never doubted of acquiring by its means an early competency, and the aim of his exertions was to secure the leisure and seclusion that should allow him to pursue inquiries into those truths that affect, to the last degree, man's nature, happiness, and destiny. He has left behind him a record of anticipated studies, whose extent and completeness have surprised even his most intimate friends.

"The character of Mr. Bellows was well known to but few. Although respected by all, for traits which the blindest must have seen, his nobler, his real nature appeared only to his most bosom-friends. It was not only for what he was, but for what he promised to be, that they loved and admired him. His intellect and heart had not yet subdued themselves entirely to his control. His affections and passions were of the strongest, and not entirely harmonized. His principles were so lofty that habit had not yet familiarized him to their constant application. Motives commanded his respect so entirely that actions went for too little with him. Christianity, which he admired and venerated, and on the study of which he had entered with no common zeal, did not produce its perfect fruits in his life; but none had wider, or more glorious, or more real views of the future state, and its great Original; none had more pregnant seeds of a lofty virtue and pure religion. None had a more rebellious spirit to subdue; few ever made greater or more successful efforts to conquer it. His character was marked by constant progress. His friends were so confident of his ultimate attainment to excellence of every kind, that they could not have loved or respected him more, had he already reached it.

"Manliness of character marked Mr. Bellows. His indomitable will, courage, and energy, rising with the occasion, carried him through every difficulty but death. With less of manliness, he had still lived. His last act was marked by his most remarkable traits. In the pursuit of duty he tempted dangers which he alone would have despised, and met death in a sleep, in which he looked only for refreshment. His strong frame would have defied disease, and he was taken away unawares. His friends may have this solid trust, that he was called home for especial reasons. He ever aspired to what the world can not give, and God was pleased to take him to heavenly springs, to slake that thirst which nothing earthly could quench."

Two families of our name and blood, whose homes were in Walpole, have been almost exterminated within the present generation, and with them, some of the fairest blossoms of our family tree.

Hubbard Bellows, his wife, and three daughters were rapidly swept from the field of life. Touching indeed was the early death of the beautiful Harriet—a name which seems an almost fatal inheritance in our family, since three lovely women have successively borne it to maturity and an early tomb. The affectionate and submissive Sophia died amid her young children, in her native village, at hardly middle life, and the younger sister, Hannah, found an untimely grave in the distant South. Their old home, the home of their father and his father, is still saddened with the desolation which has overtaken its once numerous possessors.

Col. Josiah Bellows, third son of our founder's youngest son, Josiah, was for a long time the leading business man in Walpole, and held all the various offices of trust and dignity the town and county could bestow. Handsome, well educated, dignified, and courteous, of excellent business talents, and early success—of seeming soundness of constitution and regular habits—he bid fair to be the head of a beautiful, prosperous, and long-lived race. Very early in life he married the interesting and accomplished daughter of Gen. Bradlee, and by her had four children, three daughters and one son. Who that ever knew, does not recall that lovely family? The mother's refinement, sweetness, and delicacy of appearance and manners; the daughters' various beauty as children, and ripening charms as maidens; the son's manly carriage, and frank, wholesome looks and behavior? No eye could withstand the attraction of the pew they occupied in the meeting-house; no parent behold them without a blameless envy and admiration.

But consumption was waiting for that charming group. First the mother wilted and wasted and died, bequeathing her precious memory and admirable gifts and example to her children. Then Stella, so well-named, "whose soul was like a star and dwelt apart," the pure, the heavenly-minded, the silent and contemplative eldest daughter, so motherly and so sisterly, shrinking yet reliable, spotless as the snow, diligent and faithful, uncomplaining and serene; Stella—heiress of her mother's disease, as of her name and countenance—terribly wounded by the disastrous and sudden death of her betrothed—faded away, and was no more seen. Who does not recall the angelic smile that gave its saintly beauty to her face?

Next Sarah—the tall and dignified second sister; queenly in her height and bearing; of classic regularity of feature; white as marble, and as chaste; gifted in mind as in person; lovely in character and manners—drooped and fell before the destroyer. Who can forget the bright color in her cheek, the escaped locks, the flowing figure, the radiant countenance, as mounted on horseback, this beautiful girl returned from the evening ride, amid her gay companions, and with ringing voice and laugh, galloped to her father's door? The picture—among the loveliest formed within the hills of her native village—is ineffaceably fixed in the gallery of the writer's memory.

Next Grace, early known as Rebecca, but later called, by the common consent of her friends, after the more truly descriptive of her baptismal names, followed in the sad procession! Her hair, falling in long, dark ringlets, round a most laughing and expressive face; her form pliable and graceful as a fawn's; her spirits gay as the wind; her wit quick; her heart gentle; her voice sympathetic; oh! how much beauty and goodness and animation perished with her!

Later, the only son, Rowe, who lived to marry, joined the company of victims—a frank, affectionate, transparent, and lovable young man—the idol of his companions, a gentleman by nature and breeding.

The father, bereaved of his daughters—although he lived to marry again most happily, and left one child by his second union—did not long survive his family, but died prematurely, to complete the extinction of the original household. Rarely has such a perfect blight overtaken any family; and rarely has a home left a more fragrant and exquisite memorial of itself in the heart of any community.

Finally we add to this necklace of our family jewels with which Death has arrayed himself, one fitting in lustre and worth to be its clasp. Harriet Louisa Bellows, only daughter of Abel, in maiden maturity, and in the very bloom of her loveliness, was cut off by sudden and violent illness, when at school at Lenox, Mass., in 1850. Charming in form and feature, mild and docile in temper and manners, formed to cheer and adorn the home of which she made the life and hope, this lovely girl had won the admiration and respect of the village, of which she promised to be the brightest ornament. Privileged beyond others but unenvied, an only daughter and not spoiled, beautiful but unaffected, gay yet innocent, unspeakably necessary to the happiness of her parents, Death could not spare her who could least be spared. God took her whom every body wanted, and desolated the hopes of a life; the light of a father's old age, a mother's pride and joy, an only brother's companion. Faith has consoled and time has familiarized, and a hope beyond the grave more and more lightens the dreadfulness of that loss; but it is fitting, when God smites so hard, we should recognize the full severity of his blow, though we meekly bow before his majesty and wisdom and goodness in our direst afflictions.

Of the buds of beauty hidden among the flowers of Death's coronal, which our family have lost, but which are now opening beneath a fairer sky, we can not trust ourselves to speak, since three have dropped from our own still bleeding branches. The dear babes, the sweet lambs of our family flock!—what a troop of them follows the good Shepherd over the celestial hills! God grant us leave, one day, to take them again in the arms that received them first from his hands.

It was deemed expedient, at the last moment, to give a table of the Founder's immediate family, with the names of their children. To this the author has ventured to add an account of his own immediate line, the only one he is competent to make out. The present table, however, is designed merely as a temporary substitute for one which B. B. Grant, Esq., is understood to be preparing, containing the names of *all* our Founder's descendants. This is a mere contribution to his labors, and disclaims any pretensions to thoroughness, as it does any disrespectful neglect of those branches whose names, from the author's ignorance and haste, are omitted.

The author of the Address will be permitted to say of his own father, John Bellows, born 1768, and dying at Walpole, February, 1840, that his life was one of extraordinary enterprise and success. Fitted for college, but disappointed in going by the sudden misfortune of his father, he took his fortunes into his own hands at 17, and by great activity, accumulated the means of leaving Walpole and trying his fortunes at Boston. Here, from a shopkeeper, he rose to be the head of an importing-house in a few years, (Bellows, Cordis & Co.,) and retired from business, at 50 years of age, with an ample fortune. The next ten years he devoted himself, as an Alderman of the city, to the public interests, with an almost unparalleled zeal, superintending the erection of many of the most important public edifices, and aiding, as his right-hand, the labors of that peerless Mayor, Josiah Quincy, Senior. The great crisis in manufactures largely impaired his fortunes in 1830, and he made great sacrifices (needless ones) to relieve himself of indebtedness—retiring with a comfortable estate to Walpole, N. H., where he passed ten quiet years, and died, Feb. 10, 1840, aged 72. He was a man of superior intellect, generous sentiments, and spotless integrity. Lavish in the education of his children, stern in his family government, proud and modest, tender at heart but ashamed of his sensibility, full of public spirit, unsurpassed in sharpness of wit and readiness of repartee—dignified and scrupulous in his costume and manners, elegant in the neatness of his style and his hand-writing, admirable as a letter-writer, an excellent talker, fond of speculation and argument, a keen man of business—a philosopher in his sorrows and disappointments, though easily annoyed by trifles, John Bellows (whom a thorough education would have made a very remarkable man) deserves this tribute of affectionate respect from his children, and the grateful remembrance of his fellow-citizens of Boston.

www.ingramcontent.com/pod-product-compliance
Lightning Source LLC
LaVergne TN
LVHW021417110826
845150LV00007B/1964

* 9 7 8 1 4 2 5 5 0 9 4 9 1 *